TO RUHLEBEN–AND BACK

A Great Adventure in Three Phases

Ruhleben. British civilian prisoners and their quarters.

TO RUHLEBEN–AND BACK

A Great Adventure in Three Phases

BY

GEOFFREY PYKE

❖❖❖❖❖❖❖❖❖❖❖❖❖❖❖❖❖❖

EDITED BY PAUL COLLINS

THE COLLINS LIBRARY
[A DIV. OF MCSWEENEY'S BOOKS]

McSWEENEY'S BOOKS
826 Valencia Street
San Francisco, CA 94110
429 Seventh Avenue
Brooklyn, NY 11215

www.mcsweeneys.net

The Collins Library is a series of newly edited and typeset editions of unusual
out-of-print books, and is published by McSweeney's Books.

Editor: Paul Collins
Assistant Editor: Jennifer Elder

To Ruhleben—and Back was originally published in London in 1916
by Constable and Company, Ltd.

ISBN: 0-9719047-8-2

Printed in Iceland by Oddi Printing.

ABOUT THIS BOOK

IN GERMAN, *RUHLEBEN* means "peaceful life." The roughly 4,000 British civilians interned in Ruhleben from 1914 to 1918 might have chosen a different description. Britain's entry into the Great War was so unexpected—by the British and Germans alike—that Germany on August 4, 1914 was still filled with thousands of British businessmen, visiting professors, merchant seamen, mountain climbers, music students, and even a few honeymooning couples. In previous wars they would have been deported; in this one, the men were taken to the Berlin suburb of Ruhleben, herded behind barbed wire, and left to starve and freeze for the duration of the war.

Their camp was a racecourse hurriedly converted to a holding facility: barbed wire was strung around the grandstands, and unheated dung-filled horse stables were designated as barracks. The establishment of the camp was a portent of wars no longer fought merely between armies, but inflicted on enemy civilians as well. Ruhleben was cramped and freezing, provided with insufficient food, still less medical care, and had such poor drainage that a constant latrine stink hung over the camp. And yet many Ruhleben veterans remembered their years there with some fondness. For all the hardships of the place, they were all bound together by a common identity and shared woes that erased the infamous class divisions they had known back home. Their captors did not despise them, but were simply indifferent to them; parcels and money sent from home arrived fairly unmolested, providing a vital lifeline to the outside world, and fueling a crude but remarkable economy within the camp.

In their inimitable British way, Ruhleben's internees faced abandonment in a foreign purgatory by building a little simulacrum of their homeland. Parts of the squalid camp were rechristened Marble Arch, Bond Street, and Trafalgar Square, and the barracks were as varied as London itself— Barrack 6 housed Orthodox Jews, and Barrack 13 housed blacks and Arabs. Camp inmates assembled a borrowing library, and interned professors established university classes in music and mathematics; an orchestra was formed, and a production of *The Mikado* (pieced together entirely from memory) was performed by the inmates. There was even an internal postal system complete with messengers and stamps—the camp grounds being so swampy that many were willing to pay to avoid crossing it. Among the deliveries was a literary magazine, *In Ruhleben Camp*. And, of course, each barrack formed its own cricket and soccer teams. It was, marveled the psychologist and former inmate John Ketchum, "a world so complete and many-sided that its existence in a prison camp is almost unbelievable."

Yet none of this could hide the real desperation of the inmates. Visiting diplomats and Red Cross officials were so appalled by the thousands of starving and sickly men that by 1916 Germany was embarrassed into improving conditions slightly. But it was already too late. Ruhleben had now established the German blueprint for rounding up civilians into concentration camps, which were then employed to devastating effect in the Second World War. The deadliest weapon against civilians in those camps, it should be remembered, was not the gas chamber, but sheer neglect.

One of those whose untreated illness left him on the verge of death in Ruhleben was the 20-year-old Geoffrey Pyke. Unlike every other British prisoner there, he had entered Germany after the start of the war. But Pyke was no spy. He was merely a young Cambridge student who had been brilliant at everything except his studies, and too undisciplined and unhealthy to join the military. Pyke interrupted his sophomore year to pitch a wild notion to the news editor of the *London Daily Chronicle*: Why not make him their war correspondent in Berlin? The editor called the boy's bluff, and the ever-resourceful Pyke made his way across Europe on a neutral American passport that he bought off a sailor.

After a harrowing year of internment, solitary confinement, and escape across a hostile countryside, Pyke returned home a minor hero, and was asked to write about how demoralized the Germans he'd seen were. Pyke couldn't do it. "German morale is high," he explained, "very high indeed." This is not what English editors wanted to hear in 1915. After publishing *To Ruhleben—And Back* at the tender age of twenty-one, Pyke watched as his country and his classmates were decimated by nearly three more years of war against an enemy that everyone else insisted was demoralized.

Pyke went on to lead an extraordinary life. In 1924 he founded the Malting House school, which remains a landmark experiment in British progressive education. He financed it through metal trades that at one point put him in control of a third of the world's supply of tin. The 1929 crash ended both the school and his marriage, and he spent the Depression as a destitute hermit, living on a diet of herring and broken cookies, pouring out into notebooks a torrent of ideas on everything from educational reform and film criticism to pipeline engineering. He was drawn out of hiding in 1934 when, as Hitler paid scientists to produce "evidence" to encourage Jew-baiting, Pyke rattled off a 100,000-word rebuttal to Nazi pseudo-science, and solicited backers for a foundation to critique Nazi misinformation. But he shifted his focus to organizing aid for Spanish Republicans, and neither the book nor the foundation ever reached the public.

During the Second World War, Pyke served as a scientific advisor to Lord Louis Mountbatten, the British military's Chief of Combined Operations. Officers didn't quite know what to make of him—he once proposed floating dummy ships with neon signs flashing BOMB ME, I'M A DUMMY!, the better to get Nazis to waste bombs. And yet his wartime inventions included landing craft used at Normandy, snow vehicles deployed in the Arctic, and a proposed two-million-ton aircraft carrier, hundreds of times larger than any in existence, built from a frozen slurry of wood pulp and ice called pykrete. Churchill and Roosevelt took this latter idea so seriously that the secret Habbakuk project was launched, and a prototype ice-ship built in Canada. The Allies envisioned it as giant floating platform for an invasion of Japan, and it might have become one of the largest weapons programs of the war had the atomic bomb not rendered it needless.

After the war, Pyke emerged as a popularizer of radical

solutions to daunting problems in technology and society. He was also an advocate for UNICEF and for the abolition of capital punishment in Britain, and threw himself into the genesis of Britain's system of National Health. But Pyke was dogged by poor health himself; ailing and depressed, he committed suicide on February 23, 1948. "The death of Geoffrey Pyke," lamented the *Times* of London, "removes one of the most original if unrecognized figures of the present century." His muted end with sleeping pills was, *Time* magazine remarked, "the only unoriginal thing he had ever done."

To Ruhleben—And Back was the only book Geoffrey Pyke ever published. Now returned to print for the first time since 1916, the passage of time has turned it into a curious alloy of the ominous and the high spirited. It happens to be one of the first eyewitness accounts from inside a German internment camp; that fact alone should keep it from ever falling back into obscurity again. But it has become a historical document almost by accident, because it is first and foremost a compelling tale. It is a college student's sharp-tongued travelogue, a journey of hair-breadth escapes behind enemy lines, a sober meditation on imprisonment—and, as Pyke intended, a ripping yarn.

Paul Collins
September 2002

"I wasn't afraid of something happening. I was afraid of nothing ever happening—nothing ever happening for all God's eternity."

He drained his glass and called for more whisky. He drank it and went on:

"And then something did happen. Buck, it's the solemn truth, that nothing has ever happened to you in your life. Nothing had ever happened to me in my life."

"Nothing has ever happened!" said Buck, staring. "What do you mean?"

"Nothing has ever happened," repeated Barker, with morbid obstinacy. "You don't know what a thing happening means! You sit in your office expecting customers, and customers come; you walk in the street expecting friends, and friends meet you; you want a drink, and get it. You feel inclined for a bet, and make it. You expect either to win or to lose, and you do either one or the other. But things happening!" and he shuddered ungovernably.

"Go on," said Buck shortly. "Get on."

"As we walked wearily round the corners, something happened. When something happens, it happens first, and you see it afterwards. It happens of itself and you have nothing to do with it. It proves a dreadful thing—that there are other things besides oneself. I can only put it in this way. We went round one turning, two turnings, three turnings, four turnings, five. Then I lifted myself slowly up from the gutter where I had been shot half senseless, and was beaten down again by living men crashing on top of me, and the world was full of roaring, and big men rolling about like ninepins."

G.K. CHESTERTON, *The Napoleon of Notting Hill*

PREFACE

In September of 1914, two months after war had started between Germany and England, I set out to reach Berlin in order, it is hardly necessary to add unknown to the German authorities, to act as a correspondent on behalf of the *Daily Chronicle* of London. I had also been asked to write letters for the *Cambridge Magazine*. Ruhleben was not then in existence as a prison camp, and I should certainly have had no intention of going there even if it had been. My object was to go to Berlin and see what there was of interest going on there, and then to travel across to the Rhine and the industrial districts of the West and South. I reckoned a couple of months would see the whole thing done, and that if I felt matters were becoming hot and unpleasant I would bolt as quickly as possible. It must be remembered that the desire to know the truth of what was going on at that time in the interior of Germany was intense. At the words *Krieg, Mobil,* the floodgates of news had clanged to, and not a word that could be prevented, or had not a purpose in it, was leaving Germany. At home masses of information were being produced in newspapers of all complexions, most of it contradictory, often to itself. One section of the Press told us that Berlin was a city of old men and children, of a darkness like that of Egypt and—triumph above everything else—of women tram drivers; yet when I arrived there a few weeks later one of the first things I found was young men not merely working but young men doing nothing, young men drinking, young men laughing, young men going about with young women, young men, in fact, who were committing the supreme crime of being young, while the arc lights of the Linden[1] worked as merrily as ever; and it was not until months later, in January, 1915, when I was driven across Berlin, that I saw from behind the grille of Black Maria the quintessence of German ignominy in a female manipulating a tram car. A well-known journalist with American connections told us of women clamouring for bread and screaming loudly for food outside the royal palace, yet I discovered from people who had actually been on the spot that here an isolated shout and there a lonely scream had represented the sum-total of that howling mob. Economic pressure, economic necessity, impossibility of export, necessity of export, ruin of industry—unemployment—howling mobs again— all these were phrases juggled with to make them mean first one thing and then another. But Germany was silent, and refused to show to the outside world what was going on within her frontiers, and rumours spread and grew, and phraseology grew more redundant and more pompous, and of less, and still less meaning. The German Army marched from Liège to Namur and from Namur to Mons and further, and Economic Necessity and Economic Pressure, the effect of our water-tight blockade, and again and again the howl-

---

[1] Unter den Linden, the main thoroughfare of Berlin at that time.—P.C.

ing mobs of unemployed men and bereaved women were supposed to be just treading on the tracks of the victorious hordes, about to bring the whole machine on which it depended for its life's breath crashing to the ground. It was the truth and probability of this that I set out from London to investigate, and for a time the fates were good to me, and let me wallow lazily in the sun of the Economic Pressure and Economic Necessity that were to pull down Germany to the dust; but soon they forsook me. I was caught up in the vast mechanism that has been created by, and intervenes in the lives of 67,000,000 human beings, who live within the bounds of the German Empire, and was tossed from one part to another, was beaten, crushed and hammered first by one great section and then by another, finally to be tossed aside as useless and harmless while the great machine went on its way whirring, screaming, and groaning as it worked. The way was long and weary and took long to wend. From the contemplation of itself, the machine took me and threw me into jail, and then into another jail, and then into another, and then back into the first, finally vomiting me, in a fit of either weariness, mercy or disgust, to this day I know not which, into a concentration camp for interned civilians.

This book, then, is a collection of pictures of the road thither, there and—thence. Half-way along Fate again was kind, and gave me a trusted friend in Mr. Edward Falk, District Commissioner in the Political Service of Nigeria. Together we travelled the last stretch. With him I escaped from Ruhleben on July 9th, 1915, nearly ten months after I had started out in quest of economic necessity, and to him I feel as only those who have been hunted for together, who have lain shuddering in hiding with a price upon their heads, can feel.

Unfortunately it has been necessary for me to be discreet. This I regret, because it necessitates effort. On my part to preserve discretion, and on my readers to pierce it. Had only the four and a half thousand other inhabitants of Ruhleben escaped at the same time, in a species of general stampede, and one or two other people in Berlin and elsewhere died or been killed off, matters might have arranged themselves very satisfactorily. But while the German Government follows the policy of "Vergeltungs massregeln" or "retaliatory measures," I deeply regret that on behalf of my friends whom I have left behind me I must say that discretion is the better part of valour.

G.N.P.

CONTENTS

CHAPTER I
WANTED—A CORRESPONDENCY

YES, THE GREAT MAN was in, but busy, please to wait a moment.

Æons passed, and the Great Man ceased for a few moments to be busy, and could spare a minute or so.

"Yes, yes, what is it you want? Quickly please, I've got no time to spare," and the Great Man who looked surprisingly young took up two telephone receivers, shouted instructions for foreign telegrams into each, rang a bell cunningly hid under the edge of the table, glanced about him in all directions at once, first at a row of large clock dials showing the hour in Paris, Berlin, Vienna, Petrograd, Berne, Madrid, Belgrade, Antwerp, and Amsterdam, frowned, looked at the large wall map, gave instructions to a pallid, overworked clerk for yet another foreign cable to go, and repeated, "Yes, quickly, please, I'm busy."

He truly was a great man.

Half an hour's conversation followed. The Great Man of surprising youthfulness was silent for three minutes. Then he spoke. He spoke for the remaining twenty-seven minutes. His imagination carried him along. He put one leg over the arm of his swivel chair and his hands behind his head, he got up and walked up and down. Schemes were discussed and thrown aside, details on which success or failure might depend were balanced airily and then disposed of— sometimes down one of the telephones. The Great Man was unable to make up his mind at once, he must consult, he must think, he must talk things over, he must recapitulate, he must reconsider—he must telephone. Of course to get into Germany—and out—during war was a difficult thing to do. Besides, he thought it risky. Of course, it must be distinctly understood that he could undertake no responsibility of any sort and yet the thing was most distinctly enterprising and he liked enterprise; in fact he was something of an enterprising man himself. He went on talking, and his eyes laughed as he thought of the possibility of columns of "real news" hot from Berlin or Cologne. He had nice eyes. In fact this Great Man was really the devil of a fellow. The idea of a regular column from "our special correspondent in Berlin"—our very extra special correspondent—tempted him. The possibility of success, the Great Man felt, though faint was worth it. He said "Righto! Let's leave it at that," and began talking again. For another thirty minutes he talked of what there might and might not be going on inside Germany. We rushed up and down and all over the country, and the possibility of events. Berlin—the attitude of the social democrats—especially the opinions of the large working population in the north of the city—Munich— What were the Bavarians saying?—Was it true their privileges in the imperial army system were being taken away?—What were the women saying and doing?—What impressions had the losses made?—How were our own people who had been unable to get out of Germany being treated?—Anything that was obtainable about the Zeppelins—London was going to be darkened soon for fear of them—How were the people taking the invasion of Prussia?—The main lines, Berlin, Hanover, Essen, Crefeld, Aix-la-Chapelle, something of possible interest on them all. If feasible see what Hamburg is like. How do they like the blockade? Doberitz—English prisoners. A good deal of interest was sure to arise about the young Grand Duchess of Luxembourg. There were rumours that despite all the guarantees and undertakings of the Germans she had been taken away and incarcerated in some Schloss in the interior.— Where was the Kaiser, the Crown Prince, the Empress— Prince Joachim? It was said the former had died suddenly from illness, the second assassinated, that the Empress was prostrated by the shock, and that Prince Joachim had been killed. The daily life of Berlin would also be of interest, in view of the fact that there was supposed to be neither food nor light.

The Great Man gave me carte blanche as to where I went and what I did. If I felt things getting too hot, cut and run—if there was still time. As I left the Great Man he was still talking, and the last I heard was the clatter of his feet as he stumbled over a chair in order to talk down two telephones simultaneously, and probably on different topics.

It is an odd sensation, to be in perfect safety and yet feel the fear of danger upon one, to know that nothing but at worst a motor-bus or at best a wild newspaper boy on a bicycle can do you any hurt, and yet feel the sweat stealing out from you as if already entangled in risks and dangers from which there is no visible escape. It feels queer to come from the warm busy brilliance of a newspaper office, with the telephones ringing, and passages filled with boys running here and there with proof-sheets, the organized industry of scores, to the darkness of Whitefriars Street and Fleet Street, with the cold wind blowing round one's face, and the seeming business of hundreds, all scurrying, determined-looking, ant-like, fatuous. The knowledge that to-day it is to be London and next week to be the borders of the German Empire—frontier guards, wiliness, alertness, microscopic care and precaution, food-getting and worse—news-getting, made Fleet Street look a row of ramshackle monstrosities embracing pandemonium, and oneself a regrettable ass. Everything seemed a mess. The world was in a most decided mess, the German cavalry were at most twenty-five miles off Paris, and it appeared as if they must be in occupation of the town over the week-end. London seemed hot, stuffy, grey and altogether thoroughly beastly, it was too hot to do this, it was too cold to do that, it was too damp for something else, and too dry for some other anathema, and if I did not go on this beastly German expedition, I didn't know what I was going to do. I reviewed the past and felt savage. I reviewed the present and felt worse. I reviewed the future and just managed not to explode. I was absolutely determined to be a correspondent somewhere. I remembered how I had gazed at the map, how assiduously I had examined the newspapers. I thought it possible that the ubiquitous correspondent of the papers had not been sent to Reykjavik, and I looked avidly to see if there were any messages from our special correspondent in Timbuctoo; I tried to think of arguments by which I could persuade an editor that the war was likely to develop suddenly in the Region of Lhassa of Krim Tartary. Not that I was particularly anxious to go to Rekjavick or even Timbuctoo. Lhassa tempted me not overmuch, and Krim Tartary seemed to have its drawbacks, but all the billets at the front, at Dieppe, at Paris, Bordeaux, Petrograd, and at Warsaw were full, and filled well. Suddenly it came to me. We had no correspondents in Berlin. Supreme ass of all asses—of course—Berlin; the very place; no competition; no editor could say with an air of tired resignation that he was already very well served there, and had no necessity for further assistance, though of course he was very grateful, etc. etc. No difficulty at all, except of getting there, and out again—and a day's thought ought to settle that. Of course, if the Germans were expecting English journalists to come into Germany after the war had broken out—then I should probably get caught. But the point was, were they? Would they be as wide awake as all that? If one was really careful and really wily, what were the chances? Certainly the hardest part of the problem was solved—a country of some interest was found and editors of London newspapers would not have a dozen or so corre-spondents already there. Then suddenly everything changed. Glory of glory at having something to do that seemed impossible, something necessitating all the virtues and all the vices imaginable, something for which one would have to be alert and cautious, receptive and sceptical, something that would necessitate twenty-four hours' work and twenty-five hours' watchfulness a day, and above all things the colossal humour of the idea. The fatuity of the Fleet Street crowd, the danger, the consequences, the general madness of the scheme, all were forgotten or roughly pushed aside as belonging to another being of another age, and immediately began a search that took a week for informa-tion concerning the German frontiers, and how they were guarded. It was a whirl from one end of the Kingdom to the other, chasing a man here who had got out before declaration of war, a man there who had got out by trick just after, a man released quite lately. Getting a clue here and there, often resulting in nothing but a wild-goose chase. Some knew a little, most knew nothing, one knew a lot. The whirl ceased, and I returned to town to perfect matters and to see the Great Man once more. But little more remained to be done. A book or two on Germany to be consulted, the latest files of the newspapers to be searched for any extra scrap of information, a code to be worked out for use in case of necessity, and then—off. A code if it be used frequently is a fairly easy thing to detect, though difficult to interpret. But for the first few occasions on which it needs be used the chances are in favour of its success.

Now, strange and astounding as it may seem now, one of the events the most probable for which it was most desirable to be in Berlin was for the reception of the Russians. It was known that on the incursion into East Prussia there had been something like a panic in Berlin, and it was thought that in the event of a further advance threatening there would be another—and worse. Many a paper and many an individual believed in the possibility of this firmly. It was therefore arranged that a message asking for money should be sent over the frontier, and even if caught and suspected it would convey nothing as to what it meant or from whom it came. There were roughly three directions from which the Russians might advance. From East Prussia, from Posen, or after the fall of Cracow, from the south. Their distance from the metropolis could be designated in one of three sections. The ensuing panic which these facts were sure to cause, and they were equally sure to leak out, might be put down as serious, very serious, or as a regular stampede. Primitive as this may appear, it would convey the main facts of the proximity of the Russians as known in Berlin and the effect. The Berliners' opinion as to the whereabouts of the enemy was alone likely to be of interest and importance—especially if it differed from the real state of affairs. It was a matter of no little difficulty to predict the events most likely to occur. In those days of ignorance and of bliss, of London decorated with placards saying "Breslau threatened, fall of Cracow imminent," the investment of Berlin was often discussed as a possibility within two months, and my very ingenuous self was filled to the brim with hopes that I should be the last person—most certainly the last Englishman—to leave the doomed city. The first portion of the telegram I meant to despatch the moment I was back over the frontier rose with inky vividity before my eyes. Dreams of the booms of Russian cannons on the east side of Berlin as I left it by the west came easily to my imagination; and my mind once more went back to that despatch which was to adorn, yes— I confess—I decided it was to adorn a whole page of the morning paper. Little things such as the German military and the German police did not worry me. I dismissed them as minutiæ whom I could deal with later, at my convenience. Meanwhile, however, I had to get my ticket for Newcastle.

After two days of agony on the sea, Bergen presents a great contrast to Newcastle.

The Bergen-Christiania Railway[1] is a thing by itself. It is easy to forget the maddest of mad schemes; fear and hope and all other human faculties will alike disappear before the influence of what it brings you to. Moonlight mountains,

---

[1] A rail line between the Norwegian port cities of Bergen and Christiana. —P.C.

huge lakes are but words that have been rendered meaningless by advertisements of tourist resorts, and there are no
words and never can be any that will tell of the sensation
that the fresh cold air of these great boulders, two, three,
four and five thousand feet high, the pale darkness of the
Northern night, and the lap, lap, lapping of the great lake
as it ripples backwards and forwards between one great rock
and another, give to men. Voss, where the train stops to
allow the other to pass, that comes dashing down from the
snowy heights, from amid glaciers and ice drifts, is shrouded
in darkness, but out beyond it stands this view, strong and
bold in its outline. A quietness that can be felt, a quietness
preaching the immensity of distance, closes in upon one
from all sides. The hissing of the train and all the hustling
crowd within her die away, and there is no sound beyond the
lisping of the waters of the lake, and no sight but the moon
above and its image below. The jagged line of the granite
hill marks the meeting place of heaven and earth. But otherwise all is dark, and all is quiet, and as I trudge back to
the bright-lit train, the question Why go? Why go? rings
in my ears, but as the whistle shrieks, I jump in, laughing
at the joy of doing something hard to do effectively, at the
notion of being an Englishman in Germany.

CHAPTER II
EN ROUTE FOR BERLIN

HE WAS VERY LOQUACIOUS. He was also very angry. The last
may have been the cause of the first, but I surmise that both
were produced by independent facts, and that the result of
the former was continual. He was either unmarried, which
was improbable, for he looked just the sort of man a woman
in her ignorance might call masterful and therefore marry,
or divorced, which was possible, since he never stopped
talking. He opened the carriage door with a flick of his hand
and wrist, and closed it with a slam. He stamped as if he
were on parade, and then shook himself as if he had just
come off it. He undid his belt and swung it and the bayonet
viciously on to the rack. Then he began. It was twenty-three
and a half minutes before he stopped, and then it was only
to take a breath. He seemed very happy in his anger. It fit-
ted him as well as did his trousers badly, and chiefly for the
same reason, that he was too big for both. He had a habit of
spitting at what, from a grammatical aspect, was the crucial
point of every sentence. The German Government being
largely managed by men who smoke, have, in their omnis-
cience, provided spittoons, two to every one of their railway

carriages. My friend, however, just ignored them. I drew my legs up under me. He seemed to experience a momentary surprise, and then spat succinctly right across me out of the window. It takes a long time to come from one of the northern frontiers of Germany to the capital, if you travel by bummelzug,[1] and not by the dashing through express. The police have a habit of watching that express on its arrival at Stettin, and very few of its inhabitants escape their vigilant eyes, while the bummelzug, only coming from a short distance away in an inordinately long time, necessitating an almost incredible amount of changing, has for the traveller from a distance aspects of safety and obscurity about it that make it attractive. My friend seemed to realise the time that lay at his disposal and at mine, for his next halt for breath was after thirty-three minutes. The subject of his dissertation and complaints was a "gefreiter" by name "der schweinhund," alias "verfluchte schafskopf."[2] He occasionally asked questions, or, what was the same, expected replies to statements: "So. Ach so. Naturlich. Ja, ja. Doch. Ach. So." So, all seemed to please and satisfy him. I only hoped that my interruptions uttered in a manner betokening a common sympathy between the oppressed and downtrodden against all the bloody tyrants of life, whether gefreiters[3] or unteroffiziers,[4] would not evoke questions as to my own particular martyrdom. During the turgid stream of oaths, epithets, stampings, shoutings and splutterings, I searched vainly for the cross it might be most advisable for me to be bearing in this world, should my sympathy have proved excessive, but the only thing that came persistently to my mind was the

---

[1] Slow local train.
[2] Terms of abuse.
[3] Lance-corporal.
[4] Corporal.

agony of his conversation. My next "Ja, ja. So. Doch," did not come with that blood-curdling note of pathos I put into my earlier utterances. The later editions intimated that perhaps there might be something to be said for the other side, that possibly the martyr was not so blameless as his sweating face, his porcine bristle of a moustache, and his pink neck would naturally lead one to believe. This called for argument and justification on his side to demonstrate that not merely was the gefreiter a swine, and his father, grandfather and great-grandfather swines also, but that his mother was a sow, and that, therefore, the probability was that he was not born in holy wedlock, which quite obviously put him altogether out of court. I attempted to fall asleep, but before I had come to the point when my first snore was due, he had tapped me firmly on the knee, nearly making me swear in English, which was the only thing, I believe, that would have stopped his talking of his martyrdom and his continual demands for my sympathy.

Gradually the sun began to sink, and this human organism, kept awake by passion, slipped gently into a sleep horrible to behold. And I turned from him in disgust and relief, towards the setting sun, as the train jolted shakily towards the next little station. On each side great forests of pine tree grew out of Prussia's sandy plain, and the sun glowed red between them. A mile or so and all would be barren. Fields would take the place of pine, and the sound of the hoe that of silence. It is September, and war has endured for but six or seven weeks, and already every inch of soil that before lay untouched for its poverty is now turned over and over, to prepare for the crop it must yield to its owners. The women are serious. For them work is something serious, and their sons are at the war; and even as they work a great silence reigns. It is odd how here, of all the places in Europe furthest from the battlefield, the war seems to be but behind the next hedge, and that the peasants are working in its presence in fear of it. White and anxious faces follow the letter-bag to the post office. At each village station the process is repeated, and, as the train pulls out into the distance, the village postman, generally a greybeard—for even at this early date the German Government had begun its policy of denuding the country in order to spare the towns—was to be seen trudging back to the post office, followed by all the women of the neighbourhood. To them he was the Pied Piper of Hamelin.

At a later station, as the train began to move, the monstrosity of fat awoke from his sleep in the corner with a start, shouting at me to know if this was S——. "Ja, ja," I replied, "das ist —— da," pointing to the rapidly receding platform. With a roar of awakened rage, in which he suddenly seemed to remember the porcine gefreiter, he flung himself against the door, and, wrenching open the handle, jumped down on to the line. He immediately laid his hands on his stomach, and feeling that his belt was not there, grew purple in the face as he tried to keep up by the side of the train, bawling and screaming to me to throw it to him. I reached up on to the rack, and leant out of the window with it, and he ran still faster. The next instant I had caught him beautifully right across the shins with the hardest part of the bayonet scabbard, and I congratulated myself on a remarkably good shot. I then drew in my head, leaving the somewhat befogged creature striving to surround himself with the belt. I threw myself back, delighted to have so easily got rid of what might have been a very unpleasant nuisance, chuckling at the idea that the station of S—- was as yet fifteen miles ahead.

In half an hour's time we arrived there, and, this being a spot where I had to change, I thought I might just as well start getting used to German life by having some dinner. It was some moments before I could pluck up courage to march into a restaurant, but eventually, with the *Berliner Tageblatt* tucked very ostentatiously under my arm, I strolled in. Far from being noticed by anyone, the whole world, including waiters, appeared bent upon ignoring me. Here was a quandary. My train was due to go in twenty-six minutes, and I had not eaten since the night before, when I was still the other side of the frontier. To call "Herr ober"[1] and to ask him what the devil he meant by being so slow was the obvious thing to do. Nor was it difficult. I might omit the complaints, and merely intimate by tone of voice that I was very annoyed, and that a gratuity in proportion to his speed would be his reward. My experience in the carriage had given me lessons in tones of voice, but nevertheless I felt horribly uncertain. I was now really in Germany. This was Germany, all around me. This great hall was German, this table was German, and these were Germans all around me. Ugh! What would not they say if they knew I was English. How fat that woman over there was; she would be quite presentable otherwise. Several times the words rose in my throat, but each time they failed to get further. I tried looking angry, I tried looking pathetic, hungry, helpless, wealthy, hurried, important, all to no purpose. The ober went busily on, taking a lager here, a schnitzel[2] there, calfsbraten,[3] omelet, sauerkraut, leberwurst,[4]

---

[1] Waiter.
[2] Cutlet.
[3] Roast veal.
[4] Liver sausage.

cervelartwurst,[1] schlappwurst[2] to everyone but myself. I grew angry; I grew desperate; suddenly I heard my own voice ringing out sharp and clear across the room "Herr ober." The deed was done. It was like jumping into a cold swimming bath. I had stood ten minutes shivering on the brink, but I found no difficulty when I was once in, and the ordering of my meal went smoothly, and my accent failed me not, though I was wisely laconic. I had carefully studied the prices on my menu, or speisekarte as, by the royal command, it is now called, to see if there was any rise of the price of eatables, but as I was not absolutely convinced of the ordinary price of these particular eatables, I was unable to make up my mind whether there had been any appreciable rise or not. I had carefully learnt by heart the ordinary price of a pound of beef, mutton, veal, pork, or ham, but I had forgotten to find out what fraction of a hog a pork cutlet represented, or how many ounces a mutton chop weighed. Fish I noticed on my menu had been altered to a higher price, and I was glad to feel right in the centre of Germany that the British fleet was achieving success. Yes, that dinner was certainly most fortifying. As my old bummelzug, I found, did not reach Berlin till eight the next morning, and there were no sleeping berths, I decided to go second instead of third class. I took my ticket with a whimsical feeling that if my accent was good enough for a waiter, it would have to do for a booking clerk. Nevertheless, the latter gentleman looked at me keenly before he gave me the ticket, but I stared him out of countenance and he gave me my ticket and took to examining the notes I had given him instead.

---

[1] Brain sausage.
[2] A kind of sausage.

So, so, I thought, booking clerks have orders to look at people before they give them tickets, have they. I shall have to be a bit careful. So then, in the solitude of my second-class compartment, I practised my *ch*'s diligently for twenty minutes, by which time I was indifferent as to whether they were perfect or not, as long as I did not have to rasp the back of my throat any more. All along the line strings of trucks labelled Bromberg, Thorn, Allenstein, showed that at any rate no rolling stock had been left behind for the Russians to take. Most of the trucks were filled with turnips and potatoes, though beans of various sorts were occasionally to be seen by the flicker of the station lights. The latter had been dulled, and only an occasional gas lamp served to mark, to any Russian airmen who might venture so far, the position of the railway in that great wide plain of Northern Germany.

I was kept awake all through the night, chilled to the bone, jolted to pieces by the continual shunting in order to pick up trucks at each station, which our doing duty for two trains necessitated. As dawn stole over the sky I looked out and could soon distinguish trees, fields and then houses. Gradually the carriage began to fill up, and I felt it advisable, after my experience of the previous evening with the conversationalist incorrigible, to ward off all conversation by dropping off to sleep. In a few moments a genteel suggestion of a snore tickled the ears of the clerks, shopmen, school teachers, commercial travellers, petty officials who came and went as we halted at station after station.

To enter into conversation with a stranger in a railway carriage is very nearly the crime in Germany it is in England. You are liable to be regarded as a crook or a crank, both equal objects of aversion to the worshippers of

15

ordentlichkeit[1], unless you be a university professor, in whom any vice is excused. All the inhabitants of the carriage wore that air of seriousness that pervades Germany, an air intimating that the Devil and his laughter do not exist, or that he is just about to take the hindermost. This must, I suppose, be excessively annoying to the Devil, but to an Englishman it is agony. While in England, even though death stare him in the face, it is forbidden to man to speak to a fellow-creature without an "introduction," in Germany it is forbidden by the custom of the people to give that inane suggestion of a smile that in England affords you such a kindly welcome, should you survive their frigid and aggressive stare at your insolent assertion of the right to travel, after having paid for a ticket. In Germany, it is wisest, unless you wish to appear exotic, to bury yourself in a trade newspaper, or to stare in a fashion, more bovine than considerate, at your neighbour or his boots. If you be wearing the uniform of His Majesty the Kaiser, talkativeness is permitted you, as your status can be seen at a glance, while as the poor civilian does not wear his rank or his banking account on his sleeve, there is always the risk that he might enter into conversation with somebody with whom his dignity or his cheque-book do not permit him to converse. Therefore I maintained silence. And for another reason also. Any citizen of the Empire is at liberty to cross-examine any other citizen of the Empire as to who he is, what he is, and why he is. At the commencement of the war appeals were issued to the young to help their elders by exercising their intelligence. Anyone, they were told, who might be "English, French, or Roosian" was straightaway to be taken

---

[1] Orderliness.

under a species of arrest and conducted to the nearest police station. The population of the German Empire is 67,000,000. Of these about one-half, one may surmise, are female. It is impossible, however, to gauge the proportion of boys in the other half. Possibly 99.9 per cent is an exaggeration, yet their activity was something so frightful, so intense, so Semitic[1] in its persistency that the impression of many an Englishman in Germany at the commencement of war was that there were nothing but boys behind, on the right, on the left, and in front of him, and that to the end of the war he would be unable to eat or sleep without these little angel faces looking at him, to see if he be threatening the safety of the Empire.

On one occasion I heard of a man whose grandfather had become a naturalised Englishman; his father and himself, though they had lived most of their lives in Germany, still remained English. His mother was pure German. This poor wretch was dressed in a German suit, and he had grown a beard any German professor might have been proud of, and yet, when about to take his ticket at a station he had never been in previously, a cherub of some sixteen summers walked up to him, and laying his hand upon the poor fellow's arm said: "Was sind sie für landsmann? Sie sind Englander, nicht war? Aha, so, ah," and he promptly marched him off through the town to the local police station, his features stern with pride, patriotism and duty. It was full half an hour before my friend, who had papers permitting him to leave the district on that specific day, by that particular train, could obtain his release. The boy, however,

---

[1] It is worth noting that Pyke himself was Jewish.—P.C.
[2] "What is your Nationality? You are an Englishman, aren't you?"

refused to let him out of his sight until he had left the town, and accompanied him back to the station, where they both enjoyed themselves by walking moodily up and down the platform for two hours. When the train left the station this miserable wretch, even though he had lived years in Prussia, absent-mindedly turned round and tipped that boy—twopence. He was married but had no sons. The boy rushed off to the police station again (and he had had no lunch) to report this case of bribery of an official.

A boy stepped into our carriage. I shuddered. He trod on everybody's toes and then collapsed onto the seat opposite me. We stared at each other with our intense mutual dislike ill-concealed. What he thought I was going to do to him, Heaven knows. I knew what he was going to do to me. He would start asking me questions in a loud, patriotic voice. I should reply satisfactorily, according to arrangement (mine). The rest of the carriage would then continue the cross-examination. I should foil them with the greatest ease, but the boy, being a boy and therefore not in the habit of acquiescing in the existent, would detect some flaw that his elders, including myself, were too ponderous to perceive. As likely as not he would snuggle up into the corner and console himself by merely reiterating that he was sure I was a Russian, or possibly a Jap—notwithstanding my 6 ft. 1 in. I knew there would be no gainsaying him, and if he decided I was a Jap, well I should have to be one, to the best of my English ability. If I leant out of the window, he would probably pull the communication cord, and accuse me of dropping bombs on the railway. Being a boy, and therefore unbiased, he would tell me the cut of my coat was English—though it was made in Germany—or that my boots were of Russian leather, though in truth they came from London, that my handkerchief or my necktie was Parisian—though they came from Berlin, that my felt hat was Serbian—which in truth it was. Even now I was sure he was looking me over and even through the school books which he was only pretending to study. I could see by the way his eyes wandered in a peculiarly vacant manner that he was thinking of something else. I was sure that I was that something. He would tear me limb from limb if he could. He would throw me out of the window, and then accuse me of suicide, if he thought he could prove I was a foreigner. I saw by that vacant stare in his eye and the unconscious movement of his lips as he looked at me over the top of his book that he was reciting all the crimes I was to be accused of, or the various nationalities I was to be damned with: There are such a lot that lead you straight to Hell in Germany at the present day. Yes, I was sure of it, he would give me no peace until I was safely under lock and key, and booked to face a firing squad—with himself present by special permission—the next morning. He would—- He didn't. He got out at the next station.

In this manner, then, did I enter into the city of Berlin, a humble traveller by bummelzug.

CHAPTER III

BAMBOOZLEMENT

THE FIRST THING to do in Berlin is to go to a beer café; the second thing to do in Berlin is to go to a beer café; and the third thing to do in Berlin is to go to a beer café. Not to drink beer. No. For even though the beer is light as the fluff off a dove's wing, and is served so cool, that the hot moisture of the crowded room causes the sides to drip, nevertheless it is wiser but to drink so much that you shall not be thought an unsociable curmudgeon, who buys beer and drinks it not, by your neighbours around the room. But take a sip here, and listen; a sip there, and listen again; smack your lips occasionally and loudly, and you will cast off any suspicion that may rest upon you, and will be looked upon as a temperate drinker, who enjoys his drink to the uttermost. And also you will hear many interesting things. There are two places in Germany for finding things out, one is the railway carriage, the other is the café. One soldier always talks to another, in order to compare notes as to their proximities to Hell, and Germany is all soldiers. People often travel in pairs, especially to business of a morning, and Mankind has a habit of shouting in trains, and the German has a habit of shouting over his food. For instance, just previous to the 10th of July of this year (1915) I was unintentionally informed that the High Seas fleet was no longer in Kiel Harbour—a useful piece of knowledge, had I been able to make any use of it. So I spent the first day in cafés. Berlin, I had been assured, was in a panic. "All lights out—a city of old men and boys." I listened to the men talking in cafés. I heard no despair. They were inclined to be somewhat boisterous in their lack of it. I listened to the women, and then I thought I detected a different note, though the same phrases fell from their lips as did from those of the men. It was curious how familiar everyone seemed with war, yet there was no one there who had fought in 1870. There was no one there who could even remember it distinctly. Over fifty-five years of age has a habit of staying at home, instead of going to cafés. They talked of war and nothing else, though fourteen days before, when I had landed from Denmark at Greenock, the whole population seemed to be playing golf and collecting coppers for the relief of those who were too poor to pay income tax. It was all—What was Hindenburg going to do, or what the lieutenant had said to Fritz. The Kaiser was not much mentioned. The idea that held sway in those first wonderful days, when reactionary had clasped socialist by the hand—the latter had just previously had a notice served on him that if he offered any opposition to the Government plan he would go to prison and stay there—and the Kaiser had said, amid a Reichstag frenzied with devotion—"Ich kenn kein partei, nur Deutsche,"[1] that the nation had been given not merely a born leader in their Emperor, but also an inspired strategist and organiser,

[1] "I know no party, only Germans."

had disappeared unnoticed. It was felt that though His Majesty had for years led the ship of State with but one object in his mind—unity—in the presence of this new and miraculous killing machine, the quintessence of man's creative ability, the Emperor's duty, as much as that of the humblest subaltern, e.g., Lieutenant Förstner of Zabern,[1] lay in self-effacement. Without observing it, other heroes were springing up and being created. Names never heard before in Germany were mentioned as frequently as the Emperor's in time of peace, without the recognition of a change. There was no criticism from the men. The Eiserne Kreuz[2] prevented that. In England we distinguished the exceptional in the form of the superlative. In Germany they distinguished the exceptional in the form of the incompetent. The Iron Cross is given to every man in ten. "How did so and so get the Iron Cross?" one often hears in Berlin. "Oh, he went out and held an umbrella upside down, and into it fell an Iron Cross." Thus a man who fails to get the Iron Cross is marked down as not being one of the upper tenth, and with an army of six to eight millions the number in the upper tenth is about the male and female adult and infantile population of Newcastle-on-Tyne and Sheffield added together. Now, from the day a man is born, or, at most, from the time of his examinations at sixteen to the day of his death, his status in the State and his income are, with the usual reservations as to exceptions, fixed, and it is rare that his most desperate efforts can make any change. This is a somewhat sweeping statement, but it holds good as a rule. When a man is six-

---

[1] A Prussian officer who helped impose martial law on an Alsatian town captured from France in the war of 1870; the resulting "Zabern Affair" of 1913 damaged French-German relations.—P.C.

[2] Iron Cross.

teen, he has only got to turn up a table of logarithms to find
out what will be his pension when he is sixty. The women
of Germany are these people's wives. They are not given
orders. They share those of their husbands. Frau
Geheimrath,[1] Frau Untersuchungsrichter,[2] Frau Gefängnisz-
direktor.[3] The men of Germany are ruled by a ribbon, and
the ribbon is not a woman's. For that ribbon in his button-
hole—and he never takes it off, except to change it with his
coat—a man will sell his soul. An old prison director I came
to know later on, and who had the Iron Cross of 1870
(which was hard to get then) used, I am sure, to go to bed
in it. I always imagined it pinned to his night-dress—he
was much too old to wear pyjamas—just out of the way of
his large grey beard. He must have looked quite odd dressed
like that, with a hard shiny head on top, pince-nez balancing on his stern nose, and the order heaving on his bosom.
All the independent criticism of which Germany is now full
comes from the women. The stories of placards with "Give
us back our husbands and sons," "Give us back our sons,"
are not by any means myths, though their importance has
been vastly exaggerated. The men, come what will, are bam-
boozled into being coerced, and it may yet be that the
change in the character of the German Empire will come
because its rulers forgot to bamboozle the women as well as
the men. The whole country, women included, were swept
off their feet at the beginning of all this by the question
"Will you have the Cossack in your homes?" but the women
have recovered theirs, the men have not—quite. They
seemed unto themselves as attacked by the Russian, and that

---

[1] Privy Councillor.   [3] Prison Director.
[2] Examining Magistrate.

France and then England joined in against them when they were thus beset. Their rulers commenced the war with the cry of the Cossack, and continued it on the perfidy of Albion.

And Albion with his cry of nationalities, allied with the nation that envelops in her suffocating grasp millions of unliberated Finns, Swedes, Romanians, Poles, Armenians, and above all the joint crime of Persia. Where is Persia's nationality? The Englishman and above all the Cockney is a being both remarkable and in many respects unique. For instance, the continental, and especially the Prussian, is unable to fight without either hate or enthusiasm. He must have either one or the other. He goes into battle with "Gott mitt uns" on his belt, "Gott strafe England" in his heart. He means them both. If they were absent he would at once sit down and begin asking himself why he is fighting and until he had settled on a reason in a manner thoroughly satisfactory he would cease doing so. The Englishman, on the other hand, fights as a rule without any hate or enthusiasm, and while he is deciding the question as to exactly why he is fighting he decides it is best to continue the process. "Will you have the Cossack in your homes?" they said to the citizens of Prussia. "Look what he has done in Prussia, and now when we are fighting against these waves of barbarism flowing in from the East, Albion comes and stabs us whilst in the very midst of this heroic fight, perfidiously, stealthily, hypocritically in the name of nationality. Albion, who deprived of nationality the Boers for the sake not of necessity—but of her financiers. France we can understand fighting us, have they not always sacrificed to their idea of revenge the product of their death-strewn evolution—Democracy. They the apostles of Liberty, of Equality, of Fraternity unite with the representative of suppression. But Albion!!!" The Prussians are above all a purposeful people. They have a dream and they try to fulfil it. The English don't care what they do so long as they do it in the manner of a gentleman.

It is not the docility but the independence of the German that is remarkable. If the Englishman could but stretch his imagination, so as to feel how difficult it must be to think and be otherwise than the influences around you make you, when from the day he enters the world to the day he leaves it, all that he learns, all that he sees, nearly all that he hears, and the majority of what he reads all comes or is controlled by one power with but one object. Disraeli tried to differentiate between the English method of government and the Prussian by remarking that we bamboozle the people, and that Bismarck coerced them. But in the Germany of to-day bamboozlement is the necessary corollary of coercion. It was a few days later that I heard an obviously broad-minded Prussian make the remark that the difference between the tasks of the German and English Governments, as it appeared to him, was that the first had to drive sheep and the second had to lead donkeys. With the possibility of an ultimate appeal to force, the latter is impossible without the former. Bismarck's greatness lay not in his tricks of diplomacy, or even in his unification of Saxon and Prussian, Hanoverian and Bavarian, but in his perception that this unity, that this conception of the State as a purposeful State, which he had built up, could not live unless accompanied by the control of the thoughts of the whole population. History, a subject regarded in England as of secondary importance, is taught in every school, and in the manner that the Government wish. For certificates allowing a man to teach are issued by the State, and by the State alone. The newspapers are independent, but within a limit. The first day I arrived in Berlin I was shown a notice of the Kommandantur of Berlin, forbidding the publication of *Vörwarts* until such a time as he should think fit. It was a civil matter entirely, no military information ever gets near the papers. As the educated grow up, those that are fit to pass on the coloured facts they have acquired are drawn in to the protection of the State whose bidding they serve, and from whom they draw the sustenance of life. What wonder that the leaders of thought cannot show much independence. There is one man, however, in Germany who is big enough to criticise, and yet too big to go to prison. He is not a German. His real name, which I have forgotten, ends in "ski," and his father came from Poland. But he is not a Pole. He goes by the name of Maximilian Harden, and is by race a Jew. In his paper, *Die Zukunft* (The Future), he attempts to give Germans that impartial standpoint that is the very antithesis to the wishes of the Government, who desire the man in the street to think as ordered. His language, though extremely involved—he often begins a sentence on one page and ends it up four pages on, without any anacoluthon[1]—is generally apposite. He discusses quite freely "Why is the German so disliked?" and makes long quotations from American and other foreign newspapers in an attempt to elucidate this difficult problem. I remember seeing a number, I think the March number, of his paper that had been suppressed. He attacked the Government for withholding news, and finally taxed it directly with downright lying and falsification of reports. Everybody reads the *Zukunft*, most people agree with it. Nothing happens, for nothing can happen, since their agreement is useless and academical.

---

[1] Variation or bending of grammar, for the sake of readability—*P.C.*

I wandered from one café to another. During the whole day I had a beer tankard to my lips, and viewed the world through its glass bottom. Everywhere were people talking, and in the course of that, my first day in Berlin, I heard close on a hundred conversations. Sometimes I wanted to interrupt and ask questions, but I knew after a time—that is to say by midday—I had but to move on to another café, and sooner or later I should get the information I wanted. I was particularly anxious to get some idea of how our blockade was really telling on the economic life of the country, and I knew there were sure to be cafés near the Bourse, to which business men were in the habit of going. It was necessary, however, to go into a lavatory to consult my Baedeker to see exactly where the Bourse was, as to have asked would have been next door to an invitation to be arrested, and after losing my way, and having to spend numerous pence popping in and out of lavatories, I eventually reached the type of café I wanted. I ordered the inevitable tankard of beer. I stayed in that café for forty minutes, and then I went to another close by, where I did the same. Both were crowded with business men, who discussed everything there was under the sun—except business. And as I, an Englishman, sat there amid the great big turrets of flesh, a possible Daniel in a veritable den of lions, I saw how all the prophecies so nicely indulged in, in England were wrong. I saw those cropped heads, the skin just scintillating through the stubble, the two little compact ears, and at the back those great rolling waves of fat, that surmounting the top of the collar, lolled in great laps over the edge. I saw that a country that could support so much superfluous flesh at the back of its head, could go on a long time before forced to its knees and compelled to cry pax through want of sustenance. Like camels, I murmured to myself, they will consume all this, they will live upon it. It will all be done at the allotted time, in the allotted manner. Ordentlichkeit,[1] Pünktlichkeit.[2] Have you ever noticed, oh, reader, wherein it is that the Prussians are different from other races? When you have been in Germany you will probably have noticed that the Prussian has no back to his head. By this I do not mean to say that there is just a frayed edge there, encircling a hollow, but that the whole job is finished off smoothly, as a sheer drop from the top. A Frenchman or an Englishman, and above all the Italians have a kind of bulge. The Prussian, however, continues his neck until it folds over on to the upper part of his forehead. This gives his face and his head, when viewed in profile, a parallel appearance, both rising perpendicular to unknown heights. Thus is the head of a Prussian.

[1] Orderliness.
[2] Punctuality.

A German patrol on the tender of a transport train.

CHAPTER IV

THE SECOND MOBILISATION
AGAINST THE RUSSIANS

JUST BEFORE I had got over the frontier I had been what I regarded then as singularly unfortunate, but now that I am far enough away from the workings of Fate to be able to admire her, I admit that what I had deemed misfortune was the luckiest thing that could have happened. I had been given an introduction to General von Bernhardi, asking him, if possible, to hand me on to his august master. In fact, in those far-off days of a week ago, I had chortled at the prospect of being a guest of the Emperor's. General von Bernhardi was, I knew, an old friend of His Majesty's, and invitations are freely given to the royal quarters. Whether His Majesty was on the East or the West front, it mattered little to me, and in those days, being very young, and a firm believer that everything was possible till proved the opposite by oneself, and that the madder the scheme, the better the chances of success, I thoroughly enjoyed the idea of travelling to the Imperial Head-quarters with a letter from the famous Bernhardi in my pocket. Bernhardi, by the way, is famous, but only in England. Practically nobody has heard of him in Prussia. He had a successful career in the war of

'70, and is now a snow-white-haired old gentleman of great benignity. People over there cannot see what there is in his book to make such a fuss about. It simply expresses the ordinary opinion of the ordinary army man in Prussia. *J'accuse*, even if written by a German, is quite unnecessary after General von Bernhardi's *Germany and England*.[1] It is an accusation in itself, and no better indictment of all that is bad in Prussian life could have been penned by Prussia's bitterest enemy. The only good quality that the opinions in the book possess is their ingenuous naïveté, and it is this that the military Prussian is by education, and possibly by nature, incapable of perceiving. His comment all through the book, at points that make the Englishman, whose political morality is so much higher than that of all other countries, gasp with astonishment, is "naturlich, ganz richtig so,[2] ganz richtig so," and he has no wish to waste his time reading a book that expresses nothing more than he knows at present. Nevertheless, when the opportunity arose of meeting the General, and then probably of going on to quarters quite celestial, I jumped at it. I actually had the letter in my pocket, but I was unwise in those days, not knowing that Fate, being a woman, is never to be trusted to be logical. I went to see the acquaintance in Scandinavia who had given me the note, once more before I left. To my very badly concealed disappointment he asked me if I still had the letter, and I stupidly answered that I had. His wife, or his sister, or his mother, or his aunt, or something, it seems, had quar-

---

[1] Bernhardi's 1911 book *Deutschland Und Der Nachste Krieg* (literally, "Germany and the Next War") applied Social Darwinism to argue for "World Power or Downfall," and was widely reprinted in English translation as evidence of Germany's menace.—*P.C.*

[2] "Naturally, quite right."

relled either with the General, or his wife, if he had one, and had rebuked my friend for being so tactless. If I had had any acuteness I should have lied brazenly, and said that I had posted it in advance, had I not told him the evening before, when he gave it me, that I intended calling with it at the Kriegsministerium[1] immediately I arrived in Berlin. I might have changed my mind, it is true, and posted it to Berlin, and I paid the penalty for not being quick enough at diplomacy (or lying), and had perforce to hand back the note with the best grace I could. And so closed a long vista of great and wondrous possibilities. And as I left my friend's house, I laughed to think how the Great Man would have stood on his head for three minutes, to have had an account of an interview with the Kaiser by his special correspondent. However, it is just as well, I think, that I did not get that letter, as I should have been shot, beyond the slightest shadow of a doubt, had the truth been discovered. Nevertheless, I might have been unsuspected in quarters so high, and I shall always regret that I was unable to bring off what really would have been a great coup.

But though I had missed this opportunity, I determined I would do the best I could to make up for it. I had reckoned that the Russian advance would necessitate a large calling out of reserves, and a great transference of troops, in fact, a new mobilisation. Now the main artery to the west from Berlin runs through the suburb of Charlottenburg, and just beyond Charlottenburg are the Charlottenburg woods, and just beyond the Charlottenburg woods, somewhat to the north, runs the railway. So on Sunday I took the train to Charlottenburg, and so did the whole of Berlin. Knowing

[1] War office.

that this was its habit, I knew I should be safe. And as I walked through the woods, I heard a great rumble, and then a silence that was great beside it. A long pause, and then another rumble, and I realised I was drawing nearer to it; but it died away before I reached the spot whence it came. And then I came to the edge of the wood, and over the clearing that confronted me was the railway line, and far away down the line was the great iron bridge that crossed the Havel. Keeping well within the shadow of the trees, I looked hard at that bridge, and saw what I had expected— five landsturm, two at each end, and an unter-offizier. Thus far and no further, thought I. It was from here that the rumble had come. I took out my packet of lunch, and sat down just inside the trees. I also took out two bottles of Pilsener beer from the bundle I had brought. I looked a perfect Berliner. Suddenly came the rumble again. It could not have been more than seven or eight minutes after the last had died away. In a few minutes a long train of forty-four luggage trucks had dashed past. At the rear were two ordinary carriages. The sliding doors of the vans were pushed back, and inside I saw were packed row after row of soldiers. They stood at the door, leaning out over one another's shoulders, singing cheerfully and sturdily those wonderful German marching songs that make one's very breathing keep time to them. Each truck sang the same, and right down the train— more than a quarter of a mile long—rose and fell the words of the "Wacht am Rhein." God! with what fervour they shouted it, and yet it was still music. Next would come the prayer for Franz Joseph, and next "Die beide Grenadier," and then again "Die Wacht am Rhein," and again and again, and it is the last notes that I can still hear ringing in my ears when the next train comes rushing along, and the last that I can hear from them is the same, and so on. And it remains a vista, those trucks decorated with green branches, and those jolly-looking men leaning out of them, singing, singing, singing. And all day long those trainloads of men passed and passed, and when I came back the next day they were still passing. Every ten minutes they came, and they never varied by more than twenty seconds. But the place where all this was being worked from was miles away, in a room in the Kriegsministerium of Berlin, and there, at any moment, they knew where every train ought to be, or actually was, which was generally the same thing.

It is as long ago as 1903, that the plans for mobilisation were last altered on a large scale, and it was then that they were finally moulded to their present shape. One of the fundamental necessities for the smooth working of organization to the Teutonic mentality, is not merely sheep-like docility, combined with the technical ability bred of the latest continuation school and polytechnics, but also the fact that the whole thing, or something like it, has been done before. It is generally considered safer, by superiors in Government services in Prussia, that inferiors should be able to recognise as an old friend, or tormentor, any order that should be given them. It saves them the trouble of understanding it. This was the case of the Prussian mobilisation. Every summer for the last twelve years, every station-master, the head of every locomotive depot, and every inspector in every district, every station in the Empire, received three large official envelopes, which he had already received instructions were to be put into his safe, and there kept "until they should be necessary." The first of these envelopes that disappeared behind lock and key, had inscribed on the cover in large printed capitals: "TO BE OPENED IN THE EVENT

OF WAR WITH FRANCE." On the second of these documents was printed: "TO BE OPENED IN THE EVENT OF WAR WITH RUSSIA"; and the third: "TO BE OPENED IN THE EVENT OF WAR WITH FRANCE AND RUSSIA." There was no fourth. No envelope with: "TO BE OPENED IN THE EVENT OF WAR WITH FRANCE, RUSSIA, AND GREAT BRITAIN." Every year a gold-laced official would come round to collect these envelopes, and carefully scrutinise them, to see that they were untampered with. Unfortunate station-master, or locomotive depot inspector, if they were. An organisation knows no mercy. Then, when satisfied, the gold-braided official with a sword dangling from his waist, would hand out three new envelopes, and exact receipts with solemn formality. He would pass away on to other station-masters, a silent figure, handing out three envelopes, always exacting three in return. Year after year this serious formality would be gone through; then came "the day." "You will do this, and that." "Trains will pass through your station at the following times." "Signalmen to be instructed to lower their signals so many minutes before each train." "The times for the signalmen at your station will, therefore, be as follows." "You will hand him the enclosed timetable." To the engine-drivers. "You will move out of your shed at ———." "You will maintain an average speed of twenty miles per hour." "On no account must the speed be relaxed or increased."

No engine-driver knew where he was bound for. His duty was to take his train along the lines on which he found himself, and he does so, maintaining his average speed of twenty miles an hour, his one anxiety being lest he should not "keep station," for at every important station inspectors with useless swords at their sides are sitting at telephones ready to report to the next head-quarters that train No. 206 is two minutes late. Unstopping, unstoppable, he goes blindly forward, until a signal tells him to go no further, and he may find himself relieved. All over the vast German Empire on three occasions has this happened within the last twelve months. On the day appointed, and not till then, are the envelopes torn open. For the great German General Staff knows better than anyone the value of secrecy as regards its dispositions, and it is treason to tear open any of those envelopes containing sheets with countless repetitions of "You will..." "You will..." "You will..."

It is in this manner that all of the three great efforts were prepared for months beforehand. For the last effort that cleared Galicia, it was probably March that saw a whole staff of the ablest and stiffest young men, straight from Staff Colleges, and full of ambition, sit down under the direction of a snow-white-haired old general or so, and carefully plot out with huge diagrams the exact time at which each train and each wagon was to leave its position, from where it was to be gathered in, and where it was to be concentrated, and whither it was to go. It is largely to these young men in spectacles, sitting in Berlin, that General von Mackensen owes his victories. At any rate, he could not possibly accomplish them without.

And thus noisy, and monotonous in their noise, for three days and three nights in October, and again in December, and finally in June for five days and five nights, without any sort of pause, there stole forth across the eastern plains of Germany, train after train, with just ten minutes between each, of troops or munitions, bearing death to the Russians, all unable to prepare in time defences of the same kind to stem off the avalanche that was descending upon them.

I came out again the next day and did the same thing. I strolled back to the station calculating out how many men had gone east in the thirty-eight hours that trains must have been running like that. There were about a thousand men on each; and there were six trains to the hour, and there were twenty-four hours to the day. "But," I said to myself, "they won't overburden this one line like this unless the others also are burdened in the same manner, and there are the other lines by Magdeburg and Eisleben, that could be used with the greatest ease. Therefore, allowing so many trains for stores and ammunition, half a million men must be in the process of being hurled from one side to the other. I'll remember that. I must get that home somehow." I got into an empty third-class carriage, but I was not long undisturbed. The door was suddenly flung open, and my guilty conscience caused every muscle tighten up, as I waited to see what happened. A couple of officers got in. They bowed, or rather nodded, in a curt manner to myself, and I returned it in a manner befitting a civilian. They talked for a bit, and then stopped. "What's wrong?" I thought. "Is my hat insufficiently Teutonic, or is my tie wrong?" for they both kept turning round and staring at me. As is so often the case when one comes across reality, it is so much safer, though so much more unpleasant, to be brave. I therefore returned the stare fixedly, and remarked it was a fine day, though even as I said it I could not prevent my eyes wandering out of the window to see if it had been raining. They agreed, and suddenly turned to one another and began talking again, to avoid my conversation. There is just that chance in Prussian, that, though you must not converse with a stranger as a matter of course, as you do in the Latin countries, yet you may exchange certain definite snippets concerning facts material to the comfort of travelling, such as the weather, or the beer you can get at the station of so and so. I began to take stock of the officer nearest to myself. He was a handsome-looking fellow, though not so handsome as his friend, who was a good deal older. The younger one was listening. The other was talking, like a machine-gun with a first-class man behind it, never stopping, clipping his words rather sharp at the end, though keeping his voice rather low. They still occasionally glanced towards me, and would then stop talking and look out of the window, but the vista that seemed to interest them most was myself. Once the elder one began, "Bitte——" Here goes, I thought, as I answered, "Herr Kapitän——?" But it was only to ask me to close the window. Nevertheless, they did not seem comfortable in my presence, so soon I began to emit a delicate genteel suggestion of a snore. Then they began to talk again, this time the younger one spoke. At first their words didn't reach me, and I dared not stop the gentle rasping at the back of my throat meant to indicate deep slumber. After a time the pitch of their voices rose, and some of the words came through to me. It was about the mobilisation last year. A breakdown—the Cologne bridge—Russian spies—shooting—mistake— quite young man—good Prussian family—thousand pities——" Then the train came out of the cutting in which it had been, and I could hear clearer. "Yes, then, by Jove, I was sent east to a place called Czezin, on the other side of the Karpathians. We had the devil of a time there, though we gave the other beggars as good as we got. Our fellows used to get a bit confused at first by the way the Russians fight." Here the younger one interrupted, to say he'd been stationed at Lille doing transport work since the taking of the town. "Oh, of course, of course, so you have," the elder went on.

"Oh, then, you don't know what these beggars are like. Well, the most extraordinary thing about them is the imagination with which they fight. Naturally, our organisation and efficiency knocked them out completely in the end, and they could not answer our ammunition, but they had a go or two at us first. They were always appearing exactly where we wouldn't expect them. You'd dash up with reinforcements, and they'd dash away with half a regiment's horses, and you'd get Hell from the Colonel. This was in the north by Gumbinnen, where we were for a month; I always swore to the old man it shouldn't happen again, until one day he got caught napping himself, and was taken prisoner. The same thing happened to myself later on. The whole lot of us got roped in. There were no trains to spare to take us to the rear, best luck, and so we were put under a temporary guard on the spot. They told us if we attempted to move, there would be shooting, and all that sort of thing. Our beggars drove them back later, and I managed to do a bolt. Got pinked in the flesh of my arm, as I ran. But meanwhile, I saw them managing their guns. You should have been there, my dear fellow. There these men were, great big, blond masses of humanity, handling the shell as if they had blue Hell behind them; slam would go the breech case, and almost before the shot had reached its mark, they'd have the thing open again. I'm not a gunner, as you know, but I thought they were quite sharp at it. They'd do this five, possibly six times, not often more, and then like monkeys, they would jump at the thing as if to tear it limb from limb. Pushing at the muzzle, pulling and pushing at the wheels, swinging it round bit by bit, until they get it turned, and with a rumble they tear off down the hill, and up another further along. Then once more they'd open fire, but after a while our boys did begin to get the range, and just as things were beginning to get too hot for them, their officer, quite a boy, would shout something, and there they were at it again. In fact, they often didn't wait for the officer boy to say anything, but they'd seem to know by instinct when it was time to move, and all leapt at once without any hesitation. Maybe, however, the officer boy didn't try and stop them, but just followed, knowing he would only upset the apple cart by trying to shout them back to their positions. They came back to the hill we were on, after having been to every other knoll within the three-mile radius, and had had things made too hot for them. They suddenly appeared from nowhere, and opened up at once at three thousand, fired the usual half-dozen rounds, and then found they couldn't move the gun. Then they were superb, you should have seen them. Each man became frigid with desperation. Each with his shoulder to the wheel, not a word, not a sound: just a sob as one would take a new breath, preparing for effort still greater. Our men were getting the range closer and closer, and at last one shell burst about thirty yards. I wondered what was going to become of me, and the idea that this was probably the last bit of fighting I should see passed through my mind. Then, suddenly, they broke. Their nerves couldn't stick it, so I thought. But no; now they were pulling and pushing in all directions at once, as it seemed, trying to shake the thing out of the mud it had stuck in. This time there was no silence. This time I knew that if they failed to move the beast, they really would run, for never have I heard such a shower of language. I don't understand a word of Russian, but I understood those oaths perfectly. Not a man kept his tongue quiet for half a second. Even the boy officer, who I should say had never needed a razor, his fair hands bleeding, and his legs scrambling in the dust, as he showed that last extra half-ounce he did not know he had in him, swore as profusely as any old grey-beard, steeped in wickedness. There was nothing left in them when they had got it out. They could not run, even though our last shell had wounded two men who were dripping with blood, but they rushed the thing at walking pace, till they felt better, and then they began to take the brute along at a jog-trot. I must admit I felt sorry for the fellows, when suddenly they ran up against a huge lump of rock. If they'd had horses it would have been all right, but it seems we landed a shell right among them earlier in the day, and had killed the lot." Here the train stopped at the Berlin terminus, and I "woke up" with a start. We all got up, but the elder one still went on with his description as they walked along together. And as I kept close to them, I heard him continuing: "For a fraction of a second they stopped, and I could see the savage fury that possessed each one. Suddenly, with a shout, as of seven thousand devils, they were at it again. Shoving, pulling, pushing, dragging, shaking. First they tried one side, then the other. If the wheel wouldn't go round the right side of the rock, then it must go round the left, and if it wouldn't go round the left side, it must go over the rock. If the worst came to the worst, it must go through the rock. A shrill scream from the boy in an officer's uniform, and the noise stopped. Every shoulder was pushing somewhere against the gun, including his own. It was a picture for Rodin to have immortalised in marble—an effort of the giants. Muscle and sinew strained and cracked, as backs and legs became almost as one with rigidity. A sudden shaking of the earth, and the thing had moved, and they are off once more, a jolly sweating crowd, and all I could hear as they died away into the distance, to go through again what they had already done, till Death should catch them, was one long, loud blasphemy."

Yes, my friend, I thought, you are a bit different from the men who have not yet been to the front in your estimation of the men you have to fight.

CHAPTER V

THE CRASH

AND THEN, QUITE SUDDENLY, I was arrested. I was sitting in the room that I had taken, writing my first article in the shape of a letter to the Great Man, when suddenly the door opened and in walked a tall man with a long, flowing black beard. I noticed as I looked into them that he had very beautiful eyes. He wore a dark overcoat and there were one or two stains down the front. There was another man somewhere. "Bitte, kommen Sie mit?"[1] "Aber wollen Sie nicht Platz nehmen? Wer sind?"[2] I replied, making the only attempt that my numbed brain could think of as a countermove to this direct order. The door was open and the passage was black outside. The other man stood by his side. This man's face was fat and stupid. Thoroughly pleasant and homelike—all that a wife could desire, I was sure. It looked so fat I wanted to slap it. "Dank schön, nein. Kommen Sie mit?" And then after a pause, "Jetzt."[3] Suddenly I felt I was standing with my back to the chair and that my fingers

---

[1] "Come with me, please?"
[2] "But won't you sit down? Who are you?"
[3] "Now."

were gripping it hard, I could feel my pulse in them. It was going very fast. The blood was pressing me hard round the windpipe. I could feel the air coming down into my lungs fresh and cool. I laughed shortly, and as I did so I felt that my voice would tremble the next time I spoke. "Ach, gut," I replied. But inside I could hear myself repeating, "You're in for it now. You're in for it now. Now you've been and done it. Phew... You were being shadowed after all. You're in for it now. The letter, the letter, in English too! Well, now you've been and done it. You're in for it now." And as I asked him "why"—he really had got fine eyes, dark and deep—I knew my hand was stealing out over the back of the chair—I had not noticed previously that the chair had a smooth leather back—on to the desk beyond, searching, groping for that letter. "Warum?"[1] I asked again, for I was conscious he had replied, but realised I had not noticed what. We were about six feet apart. He had just had supper, at least so one corner of his beard announced. And my hand was still groping from one side to the other for that terrible letter written in English. It must be further on, for I could feel it was neither to the left nor to the right. I dared not stretch any further back, he would notice my shoulder moving. What could I ask him? I might be able to find it within a couple of sentences. He had very fine eyes. I wondered whether any wretched criminal with guilt in his soul had been arrested by this basilisk. "Where is your authority?" I asked, and I felt pleased that the impudence of the request had made my voice firm and loud. But still I could not feel the letter, though I touched and reached and stretched for it until my biceps ached. I must get that letter. I must get that

---

[1] "Why?"

letter. To faint backwards and fall on top of it was too old a trick. They would spot it in no time. They were probably used to this kind of thing. What a thing life must be for them. Imagine the day of three meals punctuated by arrests in between for occupation, and each criminal feeling it with an intensity that life could never give either of them, not even you with those deep eyes and the leonine mane swept back from off your high forehead, until the day, when should a miracle occur you yourselves are arrested. You, you thing with cheeks like a mutton chop and a moustache like a toothbrush. You, you would... I must get that letter. I must reach it, I will. I can feel it, I can just touch it, but I can't get hold of it. I can just touch the corner of it, and the joint of my middle finger cracks as I strive to reach for it. I paw for it, like a restive horse. I scratch for it, like an irritated dog. If only I could wet my finger—but he would notice where my hand was. Minutes must be passing. Why does he stand like that? Why doesn't he say something? Why don't I? Think, think, you fool, say something—anything. Ask him why again. Remember you have still that letter to get. You are touching it now but you've not moved it yet. At any rate you've found it, which is better than minutes ago. "Here is my authority," he said, and produced a small round disc with a number and a crest on it. "So," I articulated, and I couldn't make out what my voice expressed, whether satisfaction, or doubt as to that little brass disc. "Bitte sehr, kommen Sie mit." The room was very still. I could hear no sound. "Unmittelbar,—immediately," he added. My finger was still scratching, my arm ached. I could not reach it. An inch more, a centimetre more; —I suddenly remembered the fact that there was 2.54 centimetres to the inch. "Which is sufficiently accurate for all purposes that the student is likely to come across," I could hear my brain ticking out. The dark eyes were coming nearer to mine. He was coming towards me now, he had walked a whole step. It would not be long before he had done another. In four steps he would be touching me. He would be able to see over my shoulder; see that I was doing something; see what I was doing. He would be on me like a flash. His hands would seize my arm—would twist it back. Ju-jitsu. They teach the police that sort of things in continental countries. He would call out to the other fellow. They would both give vent to long guttural "ach so," and would give a short laugh reciprocally. He had finished the second step. He was commencing the third. Life was flowing past me very quickly, my face must be very close to the stream. I could see every detail, details I had never seen before. I made my next effort for the letter, the greatest. I couldn't reach it. I ceased to try for it...

"Gut," I remarked and stepped quickly in between them for the door. They thought I was trying to run from them and took a step after me. I hit at the switch and managed to bang it out and stopped just outside. They both came out and I felt better. They had not seen that letter. But he locked the door and put the key in his pocket. "Well, that settles it finally," I said. "He's not going to put that key in his pocket, unless he's coming back to examine the place. S'pose he'll go round Sherlock Holmesing, microscope business and all that. Well, thank Heaven that won't help him much, everything's German from the dust to the dirt. But I am fairly dished as regards that letter. One thing, he did not find it while I was there. I could not have stuck the agony of it. Should I have tried to explain it away, or should I have just kept silence? What a ghastly silence it would have been!

What explanation could I have given? Well, well, that's all over. I suppose this means getting shot to-morrow morning or the next. I wonder what getting shot is like. I don't feel any effects from the prospect at present; well, I dare say I shall when it comes a bit closer to the thing itself. That'll be rather a nasty moment while they're aiming, and before the officer says 'fire.' I won't have my eyes bandaged. That'll make matters ten times worse. I should be able to feel the whole length of eternity in the dark, and the world will consist of myself. No, thanks, not for me. And how odd, they'll call it bravery or pluck or gumption or some such name. Just like they did that Florentine, L—— used to tell me of, who said if he was going to be decapitated he would certainly not be done in the ordinary way. Not he, he would put the back of his neck on the block and the axe should come down underneath his chin, on his throat. I suppose I shall feel in an awful funk when it comes to the thing itself, all kind of wobbly in the throat, and that sort of thing, and the officer in command will ask me if I've any last request to make. What shall I say?" And as I was thinking through all this a voice came out of the dark and I realised it was my friend of the face like David, who had his arm in mine. The thing with a face like a mutton chop walked along behind in bovine satisfaction and admiration for his chief.

He sometimes trod on my heels and then apologised profoundly. I took delight in shortening my stride and them suddenly lengthening it, so that he kicked it hard and had to apologise all over again. I enjoyed it. It was childish. "Where have you been to-day?" said my friend who had his arm in mine. He wore dark suede gloves. "To Potsdam," I replied, "to see the pictures. There is a remarkably fine Velasquez there." And then I found that my companion of the fine eyes knew everything there was to know about Velasquez. When not arresting criminals he absorbed himself in Velasquez. There was fervour in his voice as he mentioned the name. It was his hobby, so he told me, and it was a pleasure to him to meet somebody who took an interest in the great master. It was refreshing to be able to take one's mind entirely away from what might be termed the more pressing business of whether I was going to be shot the next morning, or what was going to happen to me otherwise. Now you, whoever you are, who are reading what I write, unless you have experienced something of the same sort of thing yourself, will regard all this as very exciting. I noticed the following day on thinking over it, and I also remember it so now, that the whole process from the moment when the quietness of my room was suddenly disturbed by the sudden rattle of the door handle to the moment which I'll describe later when I walked into a cell whose shape and dimensions I had to discover by feeling blindly with my hands, was not in the least exciting. The relations between the imagination and reality are such that the mental picture of an event may be infinitely more exciting—that is to say—if influenced by self-consciousness, and without the latter there can be no "excitement"—than when it comes to reality itself. I had thought of this scene dozens of times in a casual manner, and I had latterly avoided the thought as I found that I became "excited" under its influence, while reality left me untouched. This, as far as my own experience goes, is the psychology of adventure. My captor let go my arm, as to discuss his hobby with a prisoner was, I suppose, *infra dig.*, and to take the arm unasked of an admirer of Velasquez, was a piece of impertinent familiarity of which he could never be guilty. Thus I surmised. We talked energetically for half an hour as we wandered I knew not whither. Wishing to forget my somewhat unpleasant position, as thinking about it could do not the slightest good, I raked up all the little scrappy bits of knowledge I had about painting and invented on Velasquez opinions galore.

Soon, after passing down numbers of streets deserted except for a cold wind that caught one round the throat, we came opposite a great arch. We passed under it, and through a small side door into an office where numbers of police officers with bellies proportionate to their importance were lolling about in undress uniform and a mixed smell of stale tobacco and fresh sausage. I was told to sit down, while my captor went into another room to see a mysterious "chief." At first the lolling forms said nothing, until one turned round and said, "You'll be shot, you know," at which they all laughed great bellowy sort of laughs that seemed to originate in their intestines. They seemed to know all about me. "I don't think," I replied. I thought it best to appear to treat my own crime as lightly as possible. I had committed the supreme crime of being young and I saw that here was a rare opportunity of turning, what was really hardly my fault, all things considered, to advantage. So I laughed and asked them why, at which they all laughed also and stared bovinely at each other over lapping cheeks, and laughed again. This sort of infantile sparring went on for about twenty minutes. It was late now, and yet these portly tubs seemed to have nothing to do, except drink beer, eat sausage, turn a roaring gas still higher so that the very sausage began to sweat, and to spit contemplatively and repeatedly in a manner betokening the general good-fellowship that existed among all mankind at that moment. Occasionally one would jump up at the sound of a whistle from the inner office, and after a time bow himself out, and I could hear his repeated "Ja, Herr Kapitän," and the short sharp business-like tone of the other whom I never saw. It was not very long before my friend of the black beard appeared again. "Ja, Herr Kapitän," he said as he closed the door. "You," he said, turning to the mutton-chop face that had accompanied him before, "you will take Herr"—he paused a second and looked at me—"Herr Pyke to Alexanderplatz. You will go by cab. Have you any money on you?" "Yes," I replied. "Then you will pay for the cab." He accompanied us to the door. "Herr Pyke," he said to me quietly, "I hope it may be that we shall meet again. Adieu." He looked me full in the face. "Auf wiedersehen," I replied emphatically, raising my eyebrows interrogatively. He gave the slightest shrug to his shoulders and said, "Auf wiederse-hen—I hope." He certainly was one of the handsomest men I've ever seen. Things look bad, I thought, and turned to follow the Mutton Chop. "I must warn you," the latter remarked, and gave me a little porcine laugh, "that in war-time we carry revolvers and that if you attempt to escape,"— and he repeated the porcine giggle as he showed me the butt of an automatic pistol in his hip pocket. In the cab he at once began what I knew was inevitable—a long discourse on the iniquities of Sir Edward Grey,[1] or Sir Gry, as he called him. He paused, and then confessed very seriously that he was sorry but he must regard Sir Gry and the Devil as synonymous. "So," I replied, thinking it wiser not to be more committal, "das ist sehr interessant."[2] "Yes," he said after

---

[1] The Foreign Minister of Britain. Grey had negotiated mutual defense pacts with France and Russia, thus drawing Britain into World War I. His secretive and dissembling tactics were subsequently criticized for insufficiently deterring Germany from attacking France.—P.C.

[2] "That is very interesting."

another pause for fruitful thought, "didn't I think Sir Edward Grey a devil?" "Well," I replied carelessly, "perhaps what you say is right. Though not perhaps ein Teufel, aber vielleicht ein Teufelchen."[1] He looked at me for a moment suspiciously and then continued on the same subject—Sir Gry!

It was now nearly midnight. The cab was slow. We had already been in it for half an hour and Sir Gry had formed a never-ending topic for the Mutton Chop to discourse on in long words sparsely supplied with vowels. I tried to get him to shut his mouth. I had begun to remark, "My dear Sir, in all probability to-morrow is going to see me shot. I have no wish for the echo of your voice to waft me into eternity, so for God's sake hold your tongue"—when I remembered that my pose was that I was going to be released almost immediately, so I stopped, not thinking the two quite compatible. The horse—a euphemism—pulled one leg after the other, in dreary repetitive stumbles, until we rolled into a tremendous courtyard of red brick roofed in with green glass. It was immensely high. It was the quintessence of gloom, and of all that was windy and cold. It was Hell—done in red brick and glazed. I paid the cabman. I remember giving him the colossal tip of fifty pfennige, with the thought that money was not going to be of much use to me now and he might care to have some. My companion was impatient and asked me why I should give the cabman a tip. Did I always give tips? he asked, looking at me. "No," I replied, "I think it the most loathsome, dishonouring," etc. etc. etc.

By one o'clock, all my money, everything from a safety pin to a piece of masticated india-rubber, had been written out on a list, ticketed, and later on was taken away from me

---

[1] "Not perhaps a devil, but a devilkin."

and locked away in a pigeonhole. I was given one slip and told to take it with me. My imperial passport into heaven, I thought. I was quite bewildered by the number of passages we passed along, the doors we went through, and each was carefully unbolted and then re-locked as we passed through. Finally we found ourselves in another bureau, and here Mutton Chop handed a slip of paper over the counter, and also a vast dossier. He then remained wandering about the room, looking phenomenally stupid, his cheeks looking more like mutton chops than ever. He had been handed a receipt, signed and stamped for the delivery of myself, and I failed to perceive for what he was waiting. Suddenly a mad rush of whimsicality seemed to possess me, and as a warder came into the office to take me away somewhere, I rushed up to the Mutton Chop and pressed fifty pfennige into his hand. Then I said in a stage whisper, "Thanks awfully, ein kleines Trinkgeld,[1] ein kleines Trinkgeld." And I shall never forget his face as the warder came and took me by the arm and told me to come with him. And when a second later I looked over my shoulder back through the doorway there was the Mutton Chop gradually turning a dull purple in the light—paralysed—overcome—dumbfounded—accablé—annihilated. It was magnificent. It was superb.

[1] A small tip.

CHAPTER VI
PRISON

IT WAS QUITE DARK, and the footsteps were dying away into the distance. There was a patch of light high up on the wall, which came from a hole above the door. The footsteps had almost vanished away. Their owner wore a metal band on his heel to stop it wearing away too quick... Economy. It made a slight clang as they made pace after pace down the length of that long gallery, with its glass floor, like in the front of London shops. Everything was quite dark. There were a lot of little noises, like a hundred fiddles in an orchestra. They served to make the darkness darker. The light patch high up showed the wall was green and shiny. Nevertheless, it was a darkness that could be felt. I was somehow in great pain, but I did not know whence it came, or what it was. It was pain. There was a slight movement somewhere, where I could not tell, for it was very dark. I listened. I could hear nothing, but I knew there was noise, even though, as I say, I could not hear it. I waited; and eternity passed over me. I felt Time. My hand touched a wall on my right. I supposed I must have moved, but I had not noticed it. It was a smooth wall, but with little ruts and pimples all over it. I thought

I could hear something, and I shut my eyes, so as to listen more intently. They were useless in any case, for there was nothing that I could see with them, though they were staring rigidly into the massive darkness. The noise grew stronger. I thought it sounded very far away, and I wondered what creature of God's it was, for there was something living about it. Suddenly I knew it was quite close to me. It was going to touch me. I must not move. What was it? Everything was very dark. Still I could hear the noise; though I had to hold my breathing, for this drowned it. Then I decided the noise was a big noise far away—quite far away, and that there was nothing at all close to me. I must be calm. I was covered with sweat. Quicker than the pulsations of my heart, was the changing of mind as to where It was, whether It was near me, or far away. What It was mattered not, but Fear rushed in upon me like the rush of blood, when I no longer decided It to be distant. Now I was hardly breathing, but my heart pounded in my ears, and thundered in my brain. It was more distinct. It was loud now—quite loud. Why can't I interpret It? What is It? What is It? I have ears and I can hear It, but I don't know what It is. Oh, what is It? What is It? I leant against the wall. I waited. I could feel, and know that I was feeling, six hundred different things. I could think, and reverse my thoughts a dozen times before one half-second of time had passed through the lives of creatures far away. Eternity came and went, I knew that there was yet more to come. I must wait and let time pass...but again the noise. It was a dog. It was a dog howling softly to itself, like a child crying its heart out. It rose and fell. It changed from something plaintive and piteous. It was a howl: a howl like the moaning of a hopeless man in pain, and—alone. It breathed, and I could hear the coarse rasping of its throat, as with deliberation it pulled the air down into its lungs. But the way it commenced each howl showed it was a dog. I could imagine it, also in darkness, its head lifted on high, its eyes closed, its consciousness of life—of time and space—intense, agonising, its paws trembling in the dark, rigid, not daring to move amid the darkness overwhelming it. And then it was a child once more, moaning pleadingly for help. It sobbed, and choked, as it cried and begged for some forgiveness I knew naught of. But the prayer stayed in its throat, as with a flashing change howl after howl, each more shrill than the last, swelled up and echoed away. They grew stronger and stronger, each overwhelming the last, till they could go no further, they were so loud, so shrill. They were barked out, one after the other. I could hear no laboured intakings of breath now. The howls were coming ever faster, faster, faster. The universe was emptied of all other noise, and this alone rang through space. It was a dog. No! no! no! No dog could howl like that; it was not howling, it was screaming—screeching! It was talking! It was saying something! There was a *word* in that last howl. No, impossible. Yes. No. Yes—again and again. They were torturing someone... It was a Man. He was howling, screaming, yelling, jibbering, foaming; but why so like a dog, why? I heard the warder go down some stairs and kick at a door, and curtly order silence. The howls died down, and became a child's whimpering again. It choked, and spoke to itself. The howls grew softer... softer. They died away. There was noise; but I could hear nothing. There was movement. It was very dark...

CHAPTER VII
WAITING TO BE SHOT

IT WAS A GLORIOUS DAY when I woke up. The sun was shining brightly, and the sky was blue. It was somewhat cold, for it was still early in the morning. The consciousness of where I was gradually stole in upon me, as it had done tentatively once or twice during the night, as I met with obstacles such as the top or bottom of the bed, a couple of iron railings running down the side, a mattress at once rocky and mountainous, a coverlet that could cover nothing completely, and a wonderful triangular pillow—the shape of a slice of cake. A bell was ringing. There were a lot of noises, to which I could not fix names at the time. Then in the distance I heard a key unlocking a door. It was a double lock. Then another, and another, in quick succession. It was getting nearer; louder and louder it grew, as the person with the key pushed it hurriedly into the lock, turned it twice with remarkable rapidity, and passed on to the next, almost before the noise of the first had died away. He was saying something to each as he flung the door open. At last I could hear it at the door next to mine. Bang, bang, went my locks, and I in my shirt waited expectantly to see what would happen. Bang, went the door. "Krug heraus,[1] Krug heraus," he cried, and I leapt for the brown pitcher that I saw standing there, and placed it outside on the glass-floored gallery that ran right the way round this long, high, narrow hall. There was a space left in between in the centre, and down below I could see another row of little doors, and up above was another glass gallery, and then I could see the dull shadow of somebody's feet. It was a flash—the view of four seconds, and then the door was banged to, and the locks fell into place once more.

The place I was in was about the size of a billiard table, though probably not so long. It was high, with an arched roof; the window was six feet from the ground. the walls were painted a light green, and were shiny. About seven feet from the ground a narrow dark green band ran round the walls. I used to hate that band. Almost the whole cell was occupied by the bed—about two-thirds of its length and breadth. There was a four-legged wooden stool, and a latrine, which suddenly, by some mysterious force, began flushing as I looked at it. There were a couple of shelves at one point on the wall, and on them, arranged with meticulous neatness, were an enamel basin, a battered and dulled enamel spoon, eating bowl, salt and soap. At the side hung a comb, and a white strip of paper, the list of things, down to the last speck of dust, that had been taken from me, and which, as the list remarked, were to be returned to me, on leaving. The whole thing was really wonderful. I got down the large enamel basin and washed. The soap was a unique and sorry specimen. It had the appearance of a piece of Gorgonzola cheese nicely rounded off at the corners and carefully smoothed down at the sides; after copious rubbing

[1] "Jug outside."

an occasional bubble would be born, and a smell abominable would be generated. I used it, faute de mieux.[1] When dressed, I made my bed. It is a regrettable fact, oh reader mine, that you have not yet been sent to jail. I don't say that you ever will be, but nevertheless, while for the course of a couple of hundred pages, you and I are bound together by this odd sort of companionship, I must say I regret this fact extremely. You could understand so much better, on reading my attempts at description, what it all looked like, and above all, what it felt like to be looking at it. Imagine now, if it interest you at all to know what the consciousness of one of those creatures whom you, as a citizen and a voter of an English constituency, send to dreary months and even years of penal servitude, hard labour, and the rest of the bag of tricks, punishments that future generations will throw overboard as worthy only of the century that tolerated them; what you yourself would feel like if you were to go into your most resplendent and most luxurious lavatory, and to lock the door. For the cell in which I was placed was nothing more than a lavatory with a bed in it, and I understand they are not peculiar to Prussia. In fact, I have heard the opinion expressed that the Prussian ones are a trifle better than most. After a couple of hours you would feel rather bored. What would you feel like after a couple of months? Imagine walking up and down two and a half steps—five paces—and then back again. Imagine doing this two dozen times, and then try to imagine doing it two thousand dozen times. It is not the months that count in solitary confinement, but the quarters of an hour. Every ten minutes is eternity, and the weeks go past like days.

---

[1] "For lack of something better." — P.C.

Suddenly, I remembered that the chances were that I was going to be shot. But here, again, though I repeated the words to myself several times, and gave a little nervous laugh after each occasion, it all meant nothing to me. I found nothing in the air denoting that in a short time I was likely to be incorporeal. It seemed just as airy. Water seemed just as wet. Everything, in fact, seemed just the same. They had not even offered to send the padre along. Nevertheless, a residue of true Cambridge logic told me I was liable to it. I repeated the fact to myself several times, but discovered nothing new. It seemed too impossibly silly that I was really going to be shot. I somehow felt it did not sound quite respectable; that if I had been up at college I should have been fined for getting into a "position derogatory to the dignity of the college," that a don of sorts would have complained, that really the present generation—that the senior tutor would consider getting shot, when in an utterly defenceless position, surrounded on all sides with the barrels of rifles pointing at your heart, as something the irregularity of which appalled him. I remember thinking at this point, that after Cambridge—where, at the outbreak of war, I had been in the middle of my second year—the reality of prison was quite refreshing; though I followed it up somewhat grimly with the thought, that after the reality of prison, Cambridge would not be unwelcome. And yet nothing that I could think—the most serious subjects had as little effect as the lightest—would bring the reality of the situation within my consciousness. I felt that it was all too stupid; that there do not really exist people who would deliberately and without object, cut down a young tree just begun to grow. I seemed to have forgotten there was a war going on somewhere.

And then I remembered that I was in Germany, and I imagined myself standing, rather bewildered and inwardly feeling very forlorn, in a large hall, with a great quiet reigning, while a string of stiff Prussians, with no backs to their heads, and bellies just kept within the bounds of respectability, line in order of rank, and take their seats in a ridiculously pompous manner, ask me questions pompously, and tell me, decently, in an absolute cataclysm of pomp, that I must be shuffled off this earth as soon as pomp would allow. I am trying to give some idea of what one feels like on an occasion of that sort, and I am conscious of utter failure. I oddly enough felt no fear, though I no longer had anything distracting to occupy my attention. Having absolutely nothing to do, I was walking up and down. When about to leave King's Cross, I had felt like a hot iron searing my soul the fear of this very thing, of this very possibility, of this very moment—"the morning before."—The world is only known through the senses, and yet the merging of the individual in what, at the moment, as far as concerns him, is reality, depends possibly on the liver, the amount of sleep, breakfast, dinner, lunch, tea, wife, uncle, aunts, cousins, the strength of the light, the blood pressure in one's brain— anything—everything. But reality may be perceived—possibly fourth dimensionally—a kind of kink, not in space, but in time. It may be that the reality of a collection of circumstances is impinged upon an individual consciousness before the perception, that is to say, the five senses have received the impression, and before the brain has collated them. Unfortunately, this would involve predestination, which would be a bore.

And then breakfast came. What more could man desire? I heard it coming from a distance. Leagues away, doors were being unlocked with that extraordinary flick of the wrist: four or five, one after the other, and then shut as slowly as breakfast was taken in. In forty seconds the door would have opened, and I should have a glimpse outside again, and then in fifty seconds it would have shut again, and I should be alone with my breakfast, whatever that repast was going to be. It came: "Krug herein, herein,"[1] and I pulled in my pitcher of water, and held out my mug at the same time, simultaneously taking a diaphanous slice of bread. It was quite a feat. Then the door closed.

The Germans are a wonderful folk, as most people agree. At that breakfast at their expense they not only supplied me with bread made, not out of wheat, but out of potatoes, but also with coffee made, not out of coffee beans, but out of acorns. In fact, it can shortly be expected that they will create a substitute for water out of some other combination than that of two parts hydrogen and one oxygen.

I tried to drink the coffee. I failed. I tried again, and succeeded, though when I found my mouth chock-a-block full of some gritty substance, I had to stop. I looked into my mug, and found the bottom solid with dregs. That was enough. The opening and shutting of doors had stopped. It had passed away from me into a far-away distance and then had gradually increased as it came down the other side opposite, and then disappeared into space once more. For a moment I was under the impression that silence reigned, and then I became conscious of a number of small ingurgitatory noises from all quarters. For a fraction of a second I was puzzled; then I saw light. The prison was having its breakfast. It was very pleasing to find I had companions,

[1] "Jug inside."

and I grew quite cheerful with the prospect of seeing them. However, I thought it just as well to remind myself that, for all I knew, I was going to get shot that day or the next, and it was better not to be too cheerful, as, if it turned out to be true, I should feel the contrast. At this moment I noticed that the peep-hole in the door had moved, and that somebody had just been looking at me. A second's pause, and then the door opened and a warder came in. There was hardly room for two of us. He showed me that the bed folded up into a table, the two ends which were solid forming the surface. He was surly, but quite nice. "What was that ghastly row last night?" I asked casually, watching him closely. "Oh, that," he said. "Oh, No. 23 has got D.T. He's often been in here before. He'll go to an institution this time. It generally lasts about thirty-six hours like that. Sweep out your cell, and put the dust in the corner, and see that everything is clean, bowl, mug, soap-dish, etc." And he shut the door, and locked it. I did as he told me to; then for ten minutes or so I walked up and down, up and down. What happened next, I wondered. It was now half-past seven. I waited. It became, as I reckoned, for my watch had been taken away, five-and-twenty to eight. I waited...

At half-past eleven a bell was hit once with a metal hammer; immediately I heard funny little mice-like scurryings. Then silence. Suddenly a door was unlocked, and then another, and another, and then began that machine-gun sort of noise that I had heard before breakfast. It grew nearer, and I felt it approaching me. I leapt for my enamel bowl, in the hope of lunch. The door opened, and I thrust out my bowl. It was filled. The door closed, and the noise passed on. I used to be hungry in those days, and I ate up the pottage of beans as quickly as possible. It certainly was a large helping, and if you could get it down, you were all right for some time to come. I washed out the bowl and spoon, put them back on the shelf, and waited, waited—and went on waiting.

It had not yet struck midday, and I waited for it to do so every moment, but I was five minutes out. I was beginning to feel tired and oppressed. Suddenly the latrine flushed noisily, and then silence till the sun went down at six o'clock. Eighteen hours in a lavatory! It certainly was very exhausting.

At half-past six came tea, an exact repetition of breakfast. Then a solitary clang of the bell, and the door was double bolted. It was dark. I felt for the beaker of water, washed out the acorn dregs, and found the shelf. It was dark. I was utterly exhausted, and sitting on my stool, my head had sunk down on to the iron table between my hands. I could still just smile at the whole situation—only just. At any rate, I was still alive. They had not shot me yet. How long would they be making up their minds? How long? It was only a little past six, and though I could hear the noise of iron beds being let down, I felt that sleep would never come to me if I were to lie down now. Outside I could hear Berlin throbbing with the noise of motors and trams. I thought of all those people, free, and with lives to lead. I thought of them anxious about relatives at the front, anxious about the next meal, anxious about their own fate in the far-off future, uncertain whether they should marry somebody, cheat somebody, benefit somebody, wondering what would happen to them if they were married, cheated, or what they would do with money if left them, and if it would be necessary to return a kindness if done them by the living. I envied them their doubts. I solved their problems for them. I lived their lives for them, directing their energies. I married them; I divorced them; I was mother and father to their children; son and daughter to their parents. I gave them fortunes; I helped them spend it. I gave them poverty; I helped them bear it. I gave them politics; I made them socialists. I gave them philosophies, and made them supermen. I gave them a hundred religions, and but one commandment: Thou shalt not kill. I gave them everything they could want and took it away again immediately, that they should know its value. I gave them knowledge of good, and twice as much of evil. I created worlds, in which men lived with intensity, and any tendency towards becoming a moral and mental jelly-fish was followed with death by inanition.[1] I moulded a universe and put in it worlds other than ours, and beings unlike us, and superior to us; I destroyed it. I... I awoke with a sob, as my head slipped off my hands, and I fell against the opposite wall.

It was cold, and I knew not how late, until I remembered it was probably a case of how early. I could see one wall, because of the light patch from the beam of light coming through the hole above the door. The window also I could perceive, for the sky was bright with searchlights, probing everywhere for hostile aircraft. I clambered up at the window, and looked at these through the bars. I began to wake up. Bed I felt was impossible. I never felt less like sleep. I was very tired and I knew that I should have to get still more weary before I should find rest. Suddenly there was a complete change, and I know not how to describe it. I felt crushed by the walls. Reality rushed in upon me, and for the first time since I had left London I not merely saw, but felt,

---

[1] Exhaustion from starvation. — *P.C.*

the intense seriousness of the situation I was in. I held my
breath, and I suddenly realised I had changed to a different
being. I no longer felt immune; I no longer felt that it
would be a supremely stupid thing to shoot me. On the contrary, it appeared most obviously sensible. I no longer
regarded being shot as a somewhat humourous and possibly
a rather nervy incident in life. I felt it to be merely the first
act in something unpleasantly novel. In fact, the whole
thing, I decided, was a bore, and the sooner the matter
ended, one way or the other, the better. I suddenly found I
had forgotten all about the Great Man, and thereupon set to
work, without a shadow of justification, to curse his existence with the utmost vigour. I rushed to the door, and tried
to pull it open, but there was no handle, and I tore my nails
as I tried to insert them between it and the door-post. I
strode in two steps to the window, to see the thickness of the
wall. I counted the thick iron bars inserted there, and
longed for daylight to see if the joints at the brick-work had
rusted or loosened at all. I slapped the side wall, and then
stopped dead in case the next-door occupant should hear
me. Yes, he had: back came an answering slap, though very
softly. I was delighted. Of course, this was the proper thing
to do in prison, at least, as far as I remembered my Dumas.
I slapped again, but this time no answer came. I could not
bear to lose my new-found friend, so I slapped once more,
and a knock was again returned. It was most distinctly
intriguing. I surmised that my neighbour was in bed, and
that he was knocking with his elbow. We continued this
childish game for some time. I finally got into bed, and
whenever I felt so inclined I gave the wall a resounding
thwack, and waited for an answer. He did the same, and
whenever we felt lonesome we would thwack the walls in

mutual sympathy. It was, I suppose, to see if the other was still there, though what probability there was of either disappearing, I am at a loss now to understand.

I saw my friend the next morning when we came to put our jugs out to be filled. All that I saw of him as I poked my own head out of the door was a bare leg and foot, and about four feet up was a head protruding, and half-way between the two, a hand holding the jug. His face—a most distinct euphemism—lacked one eye, his nose was split as the result of some blow, and coagulated blood ornamented it at decorous intervals. He had not shaved for a considerable time, and then his attempts must have been with a view to copying an ornamental yew tree. All the kindness that society had left in the man overspread his battered features, in an extraordinary species of a grin. He smiled, so to speak, in sections. I imagine the battered nose in some way necessitated this. One corner would be quite refulgent with embryonic laughter, the contiguous centimetre stern with the pain that the corner created. The next millimetre would suggest humour, and the succeeding one a like amount of agony. He was toothless, and therefore appeared to be without lips, or, at any rate, if not, he grew a most bristly stubble on them. The upper stubble and the lower stubble had some difficulty in interdigitating when he shut, what I suppose, poor fellow, he called his mouth. His one eye beamed sympathy and kindness blearily, but nevertheless, in the four seconds that my view of him lasted, I had an overpowering wish to jump the pace that separated us, and to embrace him tenderly in brotherly affection. It was by pure accident that later we got a few seconds' conversation, and asked each other why we were there. I put myself down under the general head of "Politik"; he described himself as an incendiary, and added that he would probably get ten years. He said it quietly, and there was a dull sort of beseeching agony in the one eye. I said nothing; I wanted to say how sorry I was, and that I hoped he would get off after all, but somehow I couldn't manage it. I suppose I still had some of the feeling of false shame, that the education of a gentleman imposes upon Englishmen. Later on, I was to free myself from this and to learn how refreshing it is, even in a conversation that only lasts forty seconds, to be able to say you are "in" because you snatched a bag from off a lady's wrist, or because you beat or broke the bones of your wife, who is a nagging devil and you hope it hurt. It made me ponder quite a lot on the day when, after sweeping out my cell, I was told to put the broom outside, and I found somebody else doing the same who whispered, "Warum sind Sie hier?" at the same time lifting his eyebrows while he imitated picking a pocket. For a moment I hesitated, and then I nodded and whispered, "Yes." I liked the idea; I found I was liable to be considered stuck-up and dangerous if I announced myself as coming under "Politik." Respectable crime was infinitely preferable. I got rather to admire pickpockets, especially bag-snatchers. There is something really brave—not merely "sporting"—in snatching a bag off somebody's wrist, when you know that a second later there will be a general hullabaloo, and that you will be running as fast as your panting breathing will allow you, with a rabble of respectable people thundering and shouting after you. You have only got to see a real man-hunt once in your life, for all your sympathy to go to the hunted. The curious who wish to witness such will probably come across one in the streets of London one night, and it can always be seen at any really good public school.

The only unbearable people in prison are the warders, with the exception of the Governor, Respectability's sole representatives, who have never thought of committing a crime. Their virtues, such as brutality, aloofness, sneering, pin-pricking, were legion, but they could all be herded together under the splendid heading of Duty. They were not merely virtuous: they were stupid. Nine-tenths of the criminals who had not been drunkards had double their wits, thrice their originality, and a hundred times their mental and moral honesty. Even the drunkards, I should think, could give them points, when sober.

A second day had broken, and I felt partly regenerated. I ate my breakfast with magnificent self-control; that is to say, I chewed every mouthful forty times, and absolutely refused to allow each to be more than the amount of bread which could be thrust into one's mouth up to the first molar; such are the important things in a day of one's life in jail. I managed to make breakfast last for sixteen minutes (approx.). I then dusted and swept out the cell. I did it twice over, and them, pretending it was still not clean—the whole thing was speckless—I did it a third time. Then the latrine flushed.

I rejoiced at having such a clock. I would notice to-morrow morning if I finished the dusting at exactly the same moment, or if the latrine flushed later. I remember being most distinctly tickled with the fact that it was manufactured by George Jennings and Co. G.J. was now my one and only connection with the United Kingdom. Verily did I cherish his name.

Lunch came and went. Tea came and went—very quickly—and still they had not come to take me away. I heard steps approaching, and I would take down my hat and coat from the pegs under the shelf, and put the boldest face I could on the matter—quite the right sort of face to be shot in; the steps would pass my door, and I would hang up the coat and hat, and take the face off. That is to say, when steps approached, I would assume an air of lofty and confident indifference; on their passing I would return to a state of rather puzzled anxiety. As time wore on, I argued that it was getting rather late in the afternoon for shooting, and that if they had not come for me in half an hour, I might consider myself fairly safe for that day. Ten seconds later I heard some shouting from the head warder—I surmised he was head warder, because he shouted loudest and called everybody "schwein"—and heard steps approaching the door. I felt that this was It this time. I felt rather as if I was standing on the edge of a swimming bath, wondering what cold water felt like. However, they passed, and I could count on living for another twelve hours. All the morning long I had heard the warders shouting out numbers, and doors being unlocked, and their denizens taken away through the locked door at the entrance to the hall into what for all of us was a great and mysterious beyond. Later on I was to know what those continual lockings and unlockings meant. Meanwhile, the second day came to an end. I had spent forty-eight hours in this private lavatory, without books, without writing material, without artificial light, without companionship of any sort, without exercise. If this were going to continue for many days longer, I should go mad. I couldn't stand it— At least, so I thought.

CHAPTER VIII
A PRODUCT OF CIVILISATION

ON THE THIRD DAY I became convinced that if they didn't come to take me away to be shot that day or the next, they weren't going to do it at all. Why I should fix on four days as the maximum they would keep a man alive, before putting him up against a wall to face a firing squad, I know not, but I felt that the German government was not going to waste 4d. on my keep if it was going to be faced with burial expenses on the fifth day. At any rate I felt that, for my own peace of mind, it was better to fix a time after which I might consider myself safe from death, and if, after all, I turned out to be mistaken, it would be no harder to go through with the business.

I did not find this altogether an advantage, for now I had nothing on earth to think about, where before I had the joy of weighing all the pros and cons, taking first one view, then the other, abandoning and resuming both, playing with them as friends, keeping them always with me as companions. I was now also ravenously hungry. The good food I had had before being caught had prevented my feeling it very badly the first couple of days, but now, solitude and scarcity began to have their effect. I forgot all about my resolves to eat slowly, and at breakfast I pushed the bread into my mouth as far as it would go; I ate it with just as many bites as I felt inclined for. Nothing mattered as long as I got it down into my inside. When I had finished, I began to feel rather serious, because hunger—real hunger—not your going without afternoon tea, of no-eggs-at-breakfast sort of affair—can, when a man is utterly without occupation, make life one continual aching weary desire. If the desire is not satisfied, or does not abate of its own accord (as it very often does), it can have disastrous effects on a man's mind. It has been known to make men think very seriously about the rights of property, and a few have become so unbalanced as to become socialists. It used to be thought that when socialism should make its appearance as a practical force, and its value questioned, the normally filled stomachs, being utterly unbiased by want and of perfect balance, would be able to form a sound judgment on the rights of property. Nevertheless, it was a hungry man who first made the remark that property was theft. I had had previous experience of what real hunger meant, when tramping about on a few shillings a week in the North of France, and in Norway, and I knew, when one has not even a mosquito to torment one, how overpowering can become the lust for food of no matter what sort. That day I thought the mess of pottage that Esau would probably not have looked at, equivalent, if not superior, to "pêche Melba." It was not until I had finished scraping my own bowl so spotless that it was hardly worth while washing it, that I heard the whole prison echoing with everybody else doing the same. Again I had the sensation of companionship, though most of those whom I heard would never know of my existence, and I might never see them.

It was about a quarter to twelve... I had not been able to spin lunch out for more than a quarter of an hour, and I should now have to wait until half-past eleven the next day before I got my next solid meal. To-morrow I absolutely must make it last till the clock struck midday. The situation was ceasing to be humorous. I began to wonder if, granting I was not shot, I should be able to keep sane much longer. At present I was finding it rather hard to grin, while bearing it. I longed for books. I tried not to think of the hills in Norway and the plains of Normandy. I tried to forget the glowing atmosphere of the Cambridge fens. I clenched my teeth at the memory of the jolly evenings spent in the rooms of a well-known philosopher and cleric there. I rushed up and down, striding great paces. I would stare out of the window at the wall opposite. I would think of the barbarity of prison. I would... but before I had time to stop it, the thought of Cambridge, of Norway, of Switzerland, of Denmark, of France had slipped through my guard, and I was back again, spending my holidays tramping about with a rücksack on my back. Once I thought of the sea, and I went sick and dizzy with misery. The raw, intoxicating smell, and the great gusts of wind of the North Sea came blowing into my mind. And I could do nothing, nothing, but walk up and down, labouring to push these images aside. I began to have conversations with friends. They became longer; they grew interesting. I no longer walked up and down; I no longer tried to keep these images away. I sat, and the same conversation would flow and reflow through my mind until I could almost hear the voices, and could foresee the points where laughter, jibe, criticism, agreement, pause, uproar were to come. Over and over the same conversation I would go, improving it, making it more logical and more intuitive, wittier, more youthful, more energetic, more life-like. I would get half-way; I would turn back to make some alteration, review the handiwork of my imagination and then continue. Trivial were the things I thought of. I would meet a friend, and chat with him a moment, and then pass on. I would be rowing in one of the College eights, and would feel almost furious with the swearing of the coach on the bank—"Get that fat little pot of yours down, will you. Shove with your legs, don't pull with those lobster-like arms of yours. Shove, damn you, shove. You're not a blooming passenger. Do some work." And my arms almost ached as I pictured myself sweating away at an oar, and quite distinctly there appeared to me the back of stroke—for I rowed seven—and I noted the texture of his vest as the sweat oozed through it in patches, as dimly, almost unseen, the banks of the river went past me. Grassy Corner, I remember, was intensely vivid. Bow side have to pull extra hard there, to get her nose around. We neared the railway bridge; soon there would be an echo of the oars as we passed under it, and the coach, being on a bike, would disappear behind a pillar for a moment, and would start bellowing away and cursing twice as hard to make up for his absence. Again bow side had to pull a bit harder to get round the bend, again... and I almost sobbed with the pain of reality as I came back to earth. I was sweating as if I had really rowed it, and my fists were clenched between my legs as if round an oar. My legs ached, as they only can ache after rowing. My heart was racing, and I was gasping for breath. I laughed half bitterly as I got up to walk up and down once more, and found myself walking with that roll peculiar to after-rowing stiffness. It was striking midday.

*　　*　　*

I was going out for exercise. There were four or five of us being assembled at the end of the long hall. We were on the glass and iron balcony that ran right round the hall. There was another above us, and below was the ground floor. It was a week ago, one hundred and sixty-eight hours, that I had been at this end of the prison last. For one hundred and sixty-eight hours I had lived in between the four walls of that cell along there, about half-way down. I must look at the plate above my door, and see what number I am when we come back. We were supposed not to talk. The door was unlocked. Down seven flights of stone stairs we went, a turn to the right, through another locked door, and into the bureau, where an eternity ago I had tipped a member of the Royal Prussian Detective Force fifty pfennige. I still felt humorous about it.

We were five. The clerk behind the desk counted us solemnly. "Fünf Spatziergänger"[1] called our guard. "Gut. Fünf," responded the clerk, and out through another locked door we went to a dirty yard. It was a bit of a road, seventy-five paces right round. One end went out under an archway to a large yard, and a side entrance led out through a door— on to the street. Opposite both these stood a policeman with a revolver in his belt. At first we all walked funereally, five paces between each. Then I stepped off the curb, and putting all the defiance I could into my step, raced round with legs and arms flying, at five miles an hour. The two policemen, fat, blue, and authoritative, expostulated at first, and then waved their hands airily. They seemed vastly amused. I don't believe they had ever seen a man walk quickly before. The clerk, and an assistant from the bureau, came to the

[1] "Five for walking."

window and stared. I was so out of condition that I began to sweat and feel tired almost immediately, but it was impossible to give up the idea now, so I padded away as if I thought I was going to get out by doing so. As I went by the others, I would drop a whisper as I passed. "How long have you been here?... Why?... Have you seen the Direktor?... What's the number of your cell?... What's your warder like?... Any news?... Any news?... Any news?" We all thought each other spies, and were very cautious. We none of us knew why we were there, and our ignorance caused all of us mutually to affix the most horrible crimes. I was quite convinced that one man was at least a murderer. He was released the next day. "It's ghastly," one man remarked. "How do you kill time?" he whispered. "I don't," I replied unconsciously, "it kills me." I thought this such a joke that the humour of it lasted me for a whole day. I would occasionally chuckle with laughter for about ten minutes at a time, and feel a desire to tell the warder what a first-class *jeu de mot* I had given birth to.

I should explain here that this prison was the Polizeigefängnis, Alexanderplatz, the great prison where criminals, as yet merely accused, are kept before they are taken to be examined. And not really good criminals are kept here either: drunkards, vagabonds, wife-beaters, politicals, pick-pockets, bag-snatchers, were the ordinary run. Nothing so interesting as a forger or embezzler, though I once, when waiting to see the doctor, who refused to examine me because I was an Englishman, met a most charming incendiary, the second of his race, who was in for ten years. We only had a few seconds' whispered conversation, and he told me he was suspected of insanity. "Are you?" I asked, and he said he didn't think so, but of course one couldn't be sure, and then added, "since one doesn't know what sanity is."

"No," I replied, "I suppose one doesn't."

We were both quite serious. Now that I am safe here in England, I still hope for my friend, as I did then, that he will go mad. It is a much pleasanter medium in which to go through pain than is sanity. If he goes mad, he will be cared for during the rest of his life and will live among his own delusions, instead of among ours. Instead of coming out at the end of ten years into the light of the world, blinking at its strangeness, with his mind too seared and numbed even to wonder at its hard unsympathetic cruelty, he will remain in his present consciousness for ever. He, like every other jail-bird, is unconsciously doing all he can to adapt himself to his environment. He is straining to alter his nature, to deaden his ability to feel joy, as man once lost his monkey's tail for want of the necessity to hang on by it. Soon "nice" and "nasty," "pain" and "pleasure," "joy" and "agony" will all be unmeaning terms to him, and he will go about with his mind a blank, no longer able to hope, unable to feel the joy of any hope satisfied. Gradually even that numb aching background to his daily waking and sleeping will disappear, and he will become an automaton, fed, clothed, and housed at humanity's expense, a living monument to humanity itself. Ten years hence, when this which I now write has long been in the dust-consumer, and you who read it will have experienced more sensations than there are hairs to your head, will have profited by them, will have lost by them, will at any rate, have felt them, enjoyed them, or suffered under them, there will come out from under an arched door, that will clang behind him and give him not one single second's joy by doing so, a smooth-faced man. He will do nothing for a time, and he will then move off almost unconscious of the streets that he saw last ten years ago, and of which, for ten years, he has been within one hundred yards, till he blunders once more in a dull, aching misery that freedom will revive within him, into the arms of Justice, under the chariot wheels of the Law... Good luck to you, my friend. We who have passed under those chariot wheels know full well that I am wishing you the best of luck when I wish you madness, quick, fiery, strong, absorbing. (This, I would like to tell you if I could but reach you in that cell you are at this moment pacing up and down, as a message from that admirable outside world I have reached, and which you will never see with any joy in your heart, is black immorality. Your sanity, like your life, must be preserved in order that you may contemplate to the full the enormity of your crime, and the fitness of the punishment which humanity has imposed upon you. Besides, my dear fellow, society has to protect itself against you and your sort.)

I no longer even had any rooted objection to insanity. I was fast getting to that point where the doubt arises as to whether after all madness is not the true sanity. It seemed as if the really important things were those that the world ignored: that the world was really thinking huge fat thoughts about nothing and inventing yards of elaborate phrases to attach to the vacuity. I had a strong temptation to go forward and make great new discoveries of Truth in this unknown region.

That day was remarkable in another respect. A small porcine rotundity rambled methodically round the cells of those who had been there a week or more, and took down a list of the food they wanted to buy. Bread, cheese, butter were permitted. He slammed the door, and twenty-four hours later it was flung open, and out of a large basket was handed you your behests. Everything was entered in a book and checked, signed by the Direktor, and checked again; given out to the prisoners, and checked again. The book was then sent to the clerk in the bureau downstairs, and the money spent entered in each prisoner's account. They were scrupulously honest about money matters, and I remember a terrific fuss because one pfennig (1/10d.) was missing, or superfluous, or had failed to behave itself in a manner proper to pfennige. That clerk would rather have died than that he should be so inaccurate as to mislay a pfennig.

I had been in solitary confinement for about a fortnight, without books, without artificial light, without writing materials, without speaking except to the walls, when, on being gathered together at the end of the balcony at half-past two for our half-hour's exercise, which had now become a regular institution, I saw that after having varied from one to five, and back again to one, our company had now swollen to the largest proportions hitherto known to the place. The whole company, I noticed, were obviously polit-icals, and, on the whole, they did not appear German. One, indeed, dressed in a blue suit and with brown boots and moustache to match, was typical of the Prussian's concep-tion of an Englishman. For some reason—probably due to the bad food—I immediately put him down as a bounder. Why, I know not, for he turned out to be the most charm-ing fellow. When the jailer had unlocked all the doors upon his list, the main door at the end was unlocked, and we all jostled downstairs, and as we ran down we managed to exchange many a word under cover of the shuffle of feet on the stone steps. For days we were all awfully suspicious of one another, and got quite convinced that we were spies, put there by the authorities to exact confessions under the seal of fellowship. This, we all knew, was the kind of thing the Prussians would call "praktisch." I cannot remember how many we were in all, but as we went round and round that yard, we gradually closed up behind one another, until within talking distance. I got the latest news of the war. We must have closed up a bit too much, for one of the policemen shouted at us, and we had to spread out, and thus conversation for that day ended.

But the next day we continued it. Walking round and round that yard, with each of us doing his best to express angelic innocence with his face, at the same time preventing his lips from appearing to move, there would arise a gradual and gentle hum of conversation. From whence it came, it was impossible to say. Everybody was looking in different directions, and if a lip did appear to move, it was the forerunner of a violent fit of coughing. Occasionally one of the two monumental edifices would roar out, "Das conversatzion is streng Verboten. Ruhe!"[1] and a number of faces as blank as chorus-girls would turn round in complete surprise and injured innocence. Soon that subtle ethereal hum would arise again. "Ruhe," would bawl Tweedledum, "Das conversatzion is streng Verboten," would roar Tweedledee. Again that row of faces would turn with a unison that would please a music-hall manager. "Conversation... Why, who wanted to talk?"

It really was first-class sport, almost as good as trying to train a fly to do the goose step, when one got into the cell through lack of vigilance on the part of the warders. It reminded us all of that diabolic torture of schoolmasters indulged in by boys, who start all together, saying "bzzzz

---

[1] "Conversation is strictly forbidden. Silence!"

bzzzzzzz" in a pontifical undertone. The poor wretch they have set on thereupon looks up in fury, surprise, or just with a horrible sort of quietness, according to his nature and experience. Any remark on his part is met with "Noise, sir! What noise? Where sir?" or "It must have been a bee, sir, bzzz." "Ruhe!" would shout one stentor, and a dozen or so astonished faces would turn towards him. "Das conversation ist streng Verboten," would roar the other, and the dozen surprised faces would turn towards him. They both ignored this completely. We enjoyed it immensely, almost as much as do schoolboys.

After we had been taken back into the bureau, and one of our guardians had roared "Dreizehn Spatziergänger"[1] and the clerk had counted us, and replied "Gut, dreizehn Spatziergänger," we went up the eighty-five stairs and seven landings to our cells. We went theoretically in twos, but, as a matter of fact, we used to go up in a most coagulatory fashion, all talking in whispers at once. My companions were always expecting to be released the next day, for two of them were attachés to the American Embassy. They were both English, but had, at the request of the American Ambassador, taken over the management of the committee for the relief of the British destitute in Germany, and the censoring of letters sent to relatives in England via the Embassy. They, and the whole committee, all of whom were under the protection of the Embassy, were suddenly arrested one evening when at work in their office, and, except for the general suspicion of espionage, they were never told for what they were imprisoned. The two leaders received the most brutal treatment, and were in prison for, altogether,

---

[1] "Thirteen walkers."

nineteen weeks, most of the time in solitary. I saw them when they both came out. They were sorry wrecks. The others were released earlier.

After they had been there three weeks, and I had been there five, still without books and light, etc., and the days getting shorter, shorter, and shorter, they were told they would be removed to a military prison the next day. The next day was Sunday. Now, the Prussians, being firm Christians, believe that Sunday should be differentiated from other days. The prisoners, therefore, had no walk. We got up at half-past six, and waited until we went to bed again at half-past six. In addition to this, on Sunday morning at nine o'clock we were subjected to the torture of hearing German criminals from another building sing hymns. Have you ever heard German criminals sing hymns?...

That afternoon is one of those I should like not to remember. At half-past three I heard doors being unlocked, and I knew that the others were being moved to Tempelhof or some such place where they would be allowed books, etc., at least so they thought. One after another, they went past my door, and I waited for the key to be inserted into my lock. One banged my door with his shoulder as he went by. That was his adieu.

Later in the day, a charming fellow of a warder, full of deep religious feeling derived from hymn-singing with criminals, came into the cell and started jeering at me because the others had gone, "some to be released," and I had been left there. He told me I was going to be shot the next day but one. My satiric smile rather annoyed him, and, after shouting somewhat, he started smiling also, with a kind of you-wait-and-see sort of air, and so we were both left smiling at each other in this fashion, with no visible means of ever being able to stop. However, my grin was fixed, and his, after becoming somewhat feline, faded away into gloom and a hop, skip and jump, as the step of the head warder was heard approaching.

One day before my friends had arrived I had been coming up the stairs with no companion but a silent warder, when I espied a female form on the flight above me kneeling on a mat washing the steps. As I came up to her, she got up to let us pass and I saw that she had no face. I had a sudden tendency to stop and rush back, but instead I hurried past. She had eyes, cheeks, nose, and mouth, and yet there was no face. These were mere lumps of shaped flesh. There was not an expression in any of them. Her eyes were blue, but they no longer recorded even that she felt boredom. I saw that in reality she was already dead. I had passed an automaton. The warder noticed nothing. He had been there some time.

Sing Sing Prison, locking many doors with one movement.

CHAPTER IX
SANITY AND MADNESS

I FORGET NOW how many times I saw the Direktor of the prison, though at the time, the days on which I did were as distinct to me as wounds, which a man cannot see, but which he knows individually and intimately. In order to obtain audience of this gentleman, it was necessary, when the warder unlocked the door at 6:30 and the pitchers were put out, to ask to see the Herr Direktor. At half-past nine you were taken out of the cell, let through the door at the end down one flight and through to the floor which you could see over the railings of the balcony. Here again you were put into a cell, and the door was locked, and time passed by. Nothing else happened. In half an hour, or an hour, you were lined up in the passage with any others who also had requests. One by one you would go into that little office. You would bow at the entrance. "Ja?" would remark the baldheaded old grey-beard, with an Iron Cross of '70 hanging from his coat. "Ja?" And you would state your request. A vast ledger opposite him, the old bird, for he looked exactly like the Jackdaw of Rheims, would enter and sign and countersign in it. His decision was given in a curt

"Ja" or "Nein," or "Das geht nicht,"[1] and you would be standing in the line outside, among those whose chance had not yet come. You had succeeded; you had failed—who knows what luck would attend you on these expeditions. Every request to write a letter had to be made in this manner. The shiny-headed old bird, with the head jailer in attendance his hand stiffly at his sword, would enter your name, the name of the addressee, and the reason for writing it, in his vast ledger. "Ja? Nein. Das geht nicht," and it is all over. Time after time I craved permission to write to His Excellency the American Ambassador, to request him to tell my people at home that I was alive. It was granted at the third request. What agony were those mornings, pacing up and down in the cell downstairs, waiting to be put into line. What could I say to the old boy to persuade him? Hundreds of passionate words rose in my mind, as I paced up and down that cell, waiting for the moment. "Bitte, Herr Direktor, kann ich ein brief schreiben?"[2] was all that I could stammer out, almost before I had reached the threshold of his office. "Ja? Nein. Das geht nicht," and I, after staring at him with eyes like a rabbit's fastened on a snake, unable to find words to say more, aching with the dull misery of refusal, have passed away, giving the place to someone else who, in his turn, also succeeds or fails.

I used to try once a fortnight, and though I have since discovered that even the letters I wrote were never sent, yet nevertheless I always had a hope of their getting through. Regularly as clockwork every other Monday, after the Hell of Sunday, I would request to see the Direktor. For the first

---

[1] "That is impossible."
[2] "Please, Herr Direktor, may I write a letter?"

ten weeks, I persevered in this. Then suddenly I began to go to pieces. I missed one Monday, and put off asking the old bald-pate until Tuesday. When the moment came round on the Tuesday, I funked it again. Wednesday came, and again I funked. On Thursday, I managed to push the words asking to see the Direktor from between my lips. Then with a rush, realising there was no going back, I felt all courage return to me. My head became as clear as a bell, and arguments to meet every objection of the Direktor's came to my mind. He had let me write several times previously, and I had not troubled him now for seventeen days. I was confident. Again I repeated my request gently to myself... Suddenly I realised I was standing before him, and that I must speak. I must say something. I had come there to say something. Unless I asked him something, he would say I was not to be brought before him again. My eyes fixed on the large pimple on the top of his head. I could not take them away. The pimple was not quite in the centre of the cranium, but occupied, so to speak, the position half-way betwixt centre-forward and right outside. He wore it where a comedian wears a top hat the size of a five-shilling bit in attempts to be funny. My thoughts followed it. It was unique, and magnificent. "Have YOU any superfluous hair?" I thought. I should love to breathe very gently on the shiny surface, just to see if it becomes misty, or whether it still shines through everything. I wondered if it was very sensitive, so sensitive that he could feel what was reflected in it, or whether it was pachydermatous, and safe to dig pins into. He was going to move. He was just finishing off the entry he was making in the ledger. He was going to look up at me and say, "Ja wohl?"—Speak, say something—speak—speak...

It was evening. I was in my cell. The light was fading fast. I was thinking how on the morrow I would try again, how it only needed careful preparation, and I should be as able as anybody to say what I wanted to—to speak.

After you have been in solitary for some time, it becomes increasingly difficult to retain your judgment. I know that first I would make up my mind that I was going to be in prison for two years, and then a great and irresistible hope would arise within me, that I should be sent to a concentration camp called Ruhleben, that I had had a whisper of from my friends. I had hoped for some sort of a trial to know how long I was going to remain where I was. Every day that passed at ten o'clock, when I imagined that anyone, before whom I might be brought, had come down to his office, I would put on the one collar I had. Every day at six I would take it off again, preserving it for the next day. At times I became convinced that, because I was not yet of age, I was to be kept for a few months more, and that the day after my twenty-first birthday, I was to be sentenced to some ghastly sort of punishment, like solitary for two years, or for life. (There seemed absolutely no difference between these two, and I dreaded the one as much as the other. Both appeared interminable, and I had no hopes of coming out sane, even after the shorter period. I pictured myself moaning about the London Law Courts in a celluloid collar, picking up a little copying work here, and a little there, until I finally sank into a mumbling old age at twenty-five, and died in delirium tremens at thirty.)

Another fact made me terribly despondent, and fight how I would, was gradually making me utterly hopeless.

About fourteen days after my companions of the British Relief Committee had gone, a new-comer had arrived. He spoke German absolutely perfectly, but with an Austrian accent. I had heard him say something to the warder. I will not tell his story, for he is at the present moment in another prison in Berlin, though not in solitary, and is, I know, writing his reminiscences in readiness for when the war shall come to an end. Let it suffice, however, to say that he had been discovered, soon after war broke out, writing articles for a London paper. He was arrested at the flat he happened to be living in, and, after a large amount of palaver, was given twenty-four hours to leave the country in. He was accompanied to the frontier. Within a fortnight he was back again. He had gone to London, had seen his paper, had come back to Holland, and at the frontier had pretended to be an Austrian waiter who had been expelled from England. He so exasperated his interrogators at the frontier by his eternal repetition of his ill treatment at the hands of his dastardly English employers, that they finally let him pass. However, in the end he was caught—as we all are—and recognised. He had been told that he was to be sent to this place Ruhleben, and, when one day he disappeared, I naturally surmised that he had been taken there. He was very good to me, for he had managed to get permission to buy fruit; I had been refused it. So he used to buy double the quantity, and daily, on going down the stairs, smuggle me an apple. "If he," I argued, "who has done this thing *twice*, and who is hoary with old age (he was about thirty-five), gets sent to this camp Ruhleben, after being here for three weeks, and I, who have only done it once, and am not yet of age, and have been here nine weeks, and have not been sent there, then there is no hope of my ever getting there. They would have

sent me there by now, were they going to do so at all."
Afterwards, I found, of course, that he had never been sent
anywhere near Ruhleben, but simply to another prison. I
heard the most wonderful stories about his doings there, from
a friend who was sent to prison for a time. He would appear
for exercise dressed in flamboyant pink running shorts, a vest
and socks to match—and a top hat. What on earth for? Well,
if the walls of prison don't supply you with humour or whimsicality, you must undertake the task yourself.

The best of luck to him. He probably thinks I am still in
that Polizeigefängnis.

For some time I had been the oldest inhabitant of the
prison. The usual denizen of the place came for a day or two,
and then went on his way through that process called Law
and Justice. My position gradually came to give me tiny little privileges. For instance, they became quite convinced
that I was going mad, for, apart from my habit of walking
round and round the exercise yard at nearly five miles per
hour, every night I would repeat the Jabberwocky. It had
taken me a whole week with my broken-down memory to
piece together the odd bits of lines and verses that I still carried in my head; and another week to evolve Mr. Kipling's
"If." I would suddenly shout loudly into the solid blackness
that "All mimsey were the borrow-groves and the
moamwraths outgrabe," I knew quite well that borrogoves
was the correct litany, but I preferred borrow-groves; so borrow-groves it was. "One two, one two and through and
through the vorpel blade went snicker snack. He left it dead
and with its head he went galumphing back," and I would
make that "snicker snack" all slow and creepy, like Captain
Hook; and would rise to a triumphant roar as I announced
the fact that he "galumphed" back, in preference to any

other form of locomotion that might have been available, glorying at his ability to resist temptations such as taxi-cabbing, taking the tube, or walking, and, above all, the insidious run.

> "*If* you can make one heap of all your winnings
>> And risk it on one turn of pitch and toss,
> And lose; and start again at your beginnings,
>> And never breathe a word about your loss."

If (and I shouted as if I was praying for life itself)

> "*If* you can force your heart, and nerve and sinew
>> To serve their turn, long after they are gone
> And so hold on, when there is nothing in you,
>> Except the will, which says to them, 'hold on.'"

And I would repeat it softly to myself, until loudly again, pacing madly up and down the cell, I would argue, "Yes, that's all very well, you know, but your will is the very thing that suffers before your heart and nerve and sinew are anywhere near gone. Why, it's the very base, the very foundation of all things, that is attacked, and then what are you going to do, Mr. Rudyard?" Nevertheless, I found an odd sort of comfort, and they were nearly always my prayer to the setting sun as the darkness stole in.

I also used to hum, whistle and sing. This was strictly forbidden by one of the thirty-three regulations pasted on the back of the door. One night in December, when the darkness had been extra oppressive—I was in darkness for eighteen out of the twenty-four hours—and I had been singing loud enough for the warders to hear, one came up and, rapping on the door, said that such behaviour was forbidden, nevertheless, he would ask the Herr Direktor as an especial favour, if I might be permitted to whistle occasionally. This is what comes of being the oldest inhabitant of a jail. The next day there was solemnly filled into the ledger by the chief warder, and countersigned by the Direktor, "Erlaubnis zu nummer acht und fünfzig zu singen und zu pfeifen."[1]

I shall never forget the day on which, after thirteen weeks, in January, 1915, I left prison—to go to another. Nothing, I was convinced, could be more of a living Hell than those thirteen weeks at the Polizeigefängnis. I was escorted out into the street. There was snow upon the pavements: it had been summer when I saw them last. Our route lay round the corner. Here, after passing through a low door in an immensely thick wall, once again I found myself in an atmosphere, not merely of red tape, but of the very essence from which tape, and redness, are made. Those innumerable bureaux: those ticketings, docketings, searching of clothes, etc., occupied a couple of hours, until I found myself in a bright and beautiful cell thirteen feet by six. This was the famous Stadt Vogtei prison. "Vogtei," literally translated, means a bailiff's office, but why a prison should be called "The City Bailiff's Office," or why the city bailiff's office should be a prison, I am at a loss to say.

Notwithstanding the bailiff, it was quite a good prison. Large numbers of English people—five to six hundred in all—had been here before they were sent to Ruhleben "for purposes of quarantine" as the official report says. It was a gentleman's prison; it was intended for those who had sentences for minor offences to serve, e.g. two to three months.

---

[1] "Permit to Number 58 to sing and to whistle."

But this did not frighten me, as I knew of its character as a depot for Ruhleben. I was full of hope. We had two meals of skilly[1] a day instead of one. I was allowed to talk to the others during the two hours' exercise they were good enough to allow, and I could buy almost anything I wanted—bar newspapers.

I had another experience here that nearly killed me. There was the usual shelf for bowl, spoon, etc., and from the side hung a fat little book with one hundred and thirty-three rules. It contained all the punishments for all the various main crimes, worked out in permutations and combinations. Things such as "for not cleaning out of the cell for the first time the prisoner is to be punished by the three days' withdrawal of the hot meal, and a second day withdrawal of the cold meal (breakfast), or, in lieu thereof... In addition to which...or as an alternative... in substitute thereof... But for the second offence, or unpunctuality of the third degree, or dirtiness of a second degree, or noise of the twentieth degree, the prisoner shall be punished by withdrawal of... whereof... in lieu of this can be substituted..." etc. etc. Now, on the outside of this little fat book with its one hundred and thirty-three rules was a diagram of the shelf from which it hung, showing exactly in what order the washing bowl, the eating bowl, the spoon, the fork, the soap were to be placed. And not merely was there a front view, but also two side views were given: one showing the side of the shelf with one towel hanging somnolently from a nail, and the other side view showing the other end of the shelf with the booklet itself hanging even more somnolently from

---

[1] Short for *skilligalee*, the thin oatmeal gruel typically found in Victorian prisons and orphanages.—*P.C.*

another nail. But yes, there was something more: for not merely was there a picture of the booklet, but the picture of the booklet had the picture of the booklet pasted on the booklet's cover, and, what is more, the side which bore this diagram faced outwards, and the right-hand top corner was against the wall. Thus it was according to the picture. But it so happened that this was impossible, for the two were incompatible. Either the picture had to face inwards, or the left-hand top corner must touch the wall. But both together was contrary to the nature of the book. Feeling rather jolly at my new environment, I pointed this out to the jailer, who wasn't a bad sort of fellow, when he came in. At first he didn't grasp it, but when he did, he took serious note of it with pen and ink. Next day, in came the prison governor, a military-looking fellow, and he went straight to the booklet at the side of the cupboard, and examining the diagram on the cover, studied the incompatibility carefully for a long time. He turned round, and after looking whimsically at me, and them at the warder for some time, as if trying to make up his mind as to who was the biggest fool, said, "H'm," very definitely, and went away.

Alas, I only remained here five days. I had hardly finished breakfast when the warder came round with a list and said I was to "pack up," though, since I had nothing to pack, his orders were rather superfluous. Again weary hours of waiting in the bureau, and then, for the first time in my life, I saw the inside of Black Maria.

I had imagined it to have cells all the way down the side, but there were only two. There were seven of us, including a woman and a policeman. Heaven knows what the woman was "in" for, and though I several times formulated the question mentally, I could never manage to get it out. The policeman was quite a nice fellow, and let us talk, and joined in himself with an air of a busy man sparing a moment to play with some children. It soon became plain that one of the men was the woman's husband, or ought to have been if he wasn't. The others were gentlemen, sentenced for petty offences, who were being taken to the town hall to be enlisted in the army. They did not seem to relish the prospect, but "at any rate," they said, "it would be a change." I looked through the grille to see what I could of Berlin streets. There were not many people on them, and the greater number were women and in black, but the quietness of the place was nothing to what I was to see later. There were a few luxury-selling shops, such as flower sellers, that were closed, but the majority seemed able to get along. That Teutonic spectacle, extraordinary but obviously sensible, of women going about without hats could be seen everywhere. And then we suddenly drove into the inevitable yard. Two gates unbarred and locked themselves automatically as one passed. It was my third jail. It was the great prison— Moabit. A huge central hall surmounted by a dome, with wings going in all directions and the end of each wing connected by another great building, each with six storeys of cells, and each of these with its iron balcony with glass flooring. There was noise, and clanging of doors everywhere. I was told to stand at the commencement of one of the wings, just off the dome. There was a huge clock, and I noticed it had a bell attached to it. At any rate, I thought, I shall hear the hour strike. The number of my cell, I can remember it now, was 1603, "the year Queen Elizabeth died," I remarked to myself, as it was unlocked, and I went in. It was a larger cell than I had hitherto had—about fourteen feet by six. There was electric light and a table and seat that folded down from the wall. The window was, as usual, above my head, but this time it was made of frosted glass. There was a horrid suggestion of permanency about the place that made me feel rather bad. I asked the warder who gave me my prison underclothing—I was allowed to keep my own suit—whether one was always in solitary here, and for how long one came. "Immer im einzelhaft"—always in solitary—and for three to four months and upward, he said. "Never less?" I asked. "No, never," he replied. "Come with me," he continued, and I was taken down into the very bowels of this terrible edifice, till, finally, I joined a vast squad of criminals. He left me. We then filed down devious passages once more, and finally were led into a vast room with about two hundred and seventy showers in it. When bathed, I was locked into a large, bare cellar just opposite, and here I was soon joined by two others, one an elderly middle-aged man of about fifty-six, and the other an evil-looking devil of about thirty-four. They sat down on the bench. I was walking up and down. They were an interesting couple. They were about to be examined by an Untersuchungsrichter, or examining magistrate, and the younger one was coaching the other in what to say. The elder seemed too numbed to agree or disagree, though he seemed to have a tendency towards the truth, which the other promptly suppressed, but just sat there, his hands on his knees, seemingly deaf. Once the younger strode up to him threateningly as if to hit him. He ground his teeth and swore that by God, if the old man were to say that he'd—— Then he tried a different tack; he argued, he elucidated, he showed the simplicity of his ideas, and how, above all, it would help themselves.

When the young one became bellicose I had felt no inclination to help the old man. Why, I know not. I think I felt that nothing, least of all truth, should stand in the way of man's salvation from that place, and that if the old man hadn't got enough gumption to tell what seemed to be a few well-concocted lies, well, he ought to be made to, since it involved the fate of the younger man, who was not yet reduced to the state of an incapacitated jelly. It was the same old story: Fate had beaten the old man, but had not succeeded in persuading the young one that he also was beaten; the young one refused to acknowledge it. It was blind instinct that told him to lie, thought he knew with clever lawyers against him, and, worst of all opponents, the law, the chances of his getting through to freedom were remote. I had noticed hitherto that it was always the young men who felt the strain most, seemed most conscious of the inhuman cruelty of prison, and I was to find out later that it was generally the young ones who recovered easiest. Sometimes the older ones don't recover. A man I was to meet later was afflicted with sudden decay of the optic nerve, and is now gradually going blind, purely as a result of solitary.

The door opened suddenly, and they were taken out, and as they passed me I saw the younger and villainous one look at the old man, in a manner in which threats, prayers, and above all, the desire to instill the wish to live were all inexpressibly mixed. They passed. I never saw them again. I often wonder where they are. There are lots like them.

I was taken back to my cell. I was now sinking fast. I saw little hope of recovery. I was quickly becoming a broken-down creature, and though physically I should have lasted out for years, mentally I saw there was a crash not far ahead. I had seen it happen with other men before. As it was, mentally I was fast becoming a species of cow. I would stand for hours at a time, leaning my head into the corner, my hands in my pockets, staring at the floor. I would find that for hours I had been saying to myself "My dear sir"—I always called myself "my dear sir" when talking out loud— "you really must make an effort to get out. I mean it's simply too stupid to spend the best years of your life in a box like this. Use your wits. Do something. Go on, you juggins, get out somewhere. Think!" and so on, from twelve till three. I became absolutely impersonal, and found it difficult to have likes and dislikes about anything. I absolutely forgot what flowers smelt like. Milk I could not imagine. Fruit, tobacco, fish, were mere names to me. I had forgotten what they were. I could not understand the meaning of the term "red."

Though I longed to be free, I felt that human beings would be perfectly unbearable. I no longer considered myself as one. I felt perfectly decorporealised: I was merely a mind contemplative and a poor one at that. And yet I longed for their company. I still kept up my nightly habit of repeating a few verses from any poem I could remember, and after the light had gone out—for here there was electric light—I would rise solemnly in the dark, and make the most fiery of speeches to the Cambridge Union—poor Cambridge Union. I would then proceed to oppose my own motion, pick holes in it, show up the proposer as an impostor and a charlatan. A seconder would then arise, who with all the sarcasm of a Voltaire would rend the immediate speaker adjective from substantive, verb from adverb, until quivering with the laceration received, the latter would be thrown, a bleeding proposition, into the waste deserts of verbosity.

It was just about this time that I nearly got myself shot for attempted murder. I was so used to the darkness that I found electric light rather trying to the eyes, and therefore

turned the bracket upwards toward the ceiling in order to
have but reflected light. A little later in came the warder. He
saw the upturned bracket, and lifting the hilt of his sword,
hit me sharply over the head. In a flash I was on him. I had
raised my fists on each side for a smashing blow on his temples. He was unable to get away, for he was so short that my
arms could have nailed him as he tried. He saw there was no
escape, and the sight of my face blazing with fury and
wretchedness made him drop his sword. I relished that
moment, I gloated over it. I kept my fists going backwards
and forwards nearly touching his temples, but never quite. I
tried to imagine the agony in his rabbit-like mind, waiting
for the crushing blow to fall upon him, and wondering what
it would feel like. Suddenly he turned a sickly green. His hat
was knocked all on one side. I saw beneath his uniform a fat
little vulgar bourgeois, incapable of a thought outside the
satisfying of his own senses. He turned from green to a pasty
yellow. He glanced piteously up into my distorted face. I
drove him back towards the door, growling and hissing at
him, my fists going like a steam hammer on each side of his
head. His agony became worse. His eyes flew from one side
to the other, like a rabbit looking for escape. His little pointed flaxen beard wobbled and, such was his panic, so did his
stomach. Suddenly my mind changed, and taking him by
the shoulders, and putting my knee, as far as it was possible,
into his belly, I pushed him backwards, and he sat down violently and disconsolately in the passage outside, his sword
underneath him, and his hat rolling away into the darkness.
I slammed the door, and after a time he got up and locked it,
I knew nothing would happen to me, for he was not permitted to hit me, but had I hit him back, I gasp to think of the
number of years I should now be doing.

This, the third prison I had been in, was the worst. Physically it was slightly better: there was more space, light, two good meals a day, but the very last drop of individuality was taken away from you. It was not permitted even to arrange the bowls on the shelf as you liked. I never saw daylight, for our exercise took place at half-past six in the dark. It was now the 20th of January: I had been arrested in the early days of October. Since them I had been residing in a lavatory. I found it dull.

Despite the warder's announcement that nobody ever came there for less than three of four months, I was suddenly taken away again after five days, and Black Maria drove me back once more to the Polizeigefängnis of the Alexanderplatz. I was too miserable by now to care where I was sent or what they did to me. I was beginning to lose the power of appreciating anything—whatever its nature. I found some new arrivals at Alexanderplatz. The place was full as usual with neutrals who were under suspicion: Dutch, Swedes and Danes. One Dutchman had been there for seven weeks in solitary. I was just reaching the final depths of despair when, one night, just as I had got my first foot into bed, the door was flung open, and into the gloom a voice shouted "raus."[1] I "raused" timidly and in my night-shirt, and was told to dress quickly. I did so, surmising I was to go to another prison. I began to feel quite numb, and I no longer hoped for anything. Downstairs in the bureau a very pleasant policeman took charge of me, and after having signed the receipts for the acceptance of my carcase, he made the usual remark, "Kommen Sie mit," and off we went. I thought it odd that we should go alone: they usually fetch

[1] "Out."

the criminals in batches. "Where are we going to?" I asked. "Ruhleben," he said.

For a moment I could hardly feel. I hardly dared feel. I just breathed quietly to myself, and thought how nice the air tasted. I was going to see human beings again. For a time the words were rather meaningless, and then I gradually began to revive under their warmth. We went out into the street to the Alexanderplatz station. I had a fine opportunity to run away here, though I should have been a fool to have done so, and to have invited prison again. In any case, I had no glasses with me, and I was very short-sighted. We had gone up on to the platform, and I was chuckling and giggling like a schoolgirl at seeing life once again, when the policeman discovered it was the wrong one. "Run," he said, "there's our train over there." I ran like a leopard. In ten bounds I had slipped through the crowd and had lost him. I ran on down the stairs, and into the street. How glorious it all seemed, and I roared aloud with laughter, at which a sallow-faced woman in black seemed offended and turned round to stare. I rushed on, up the other set of stairs and in time my captor appeared. The idea of bolting had just entered my head and flown, but "no," I said, "wait till we get to Ruhleben, and have got tired of that, then we'll see what can be done."

Meanwhile, I stared out into the darkness from the brightly lit carriage as we steamed through the suburbs of Berlin. I got a glimpse of a tiny room, in which numbers of steaming dishevelled women were crowded together bending over machines and needlework. They were being sweated. That was their daily life. They, too, lived in what was really a prison, though no law stopped them roaming whence they would. I was in the world once more...

CHAPTER X

THE IMPRESSIONS OF A LUNATIC
ON RELEASE FROM SOLITARY

SO MUCH HAS BEEN WRITTEN about Ruhleben; so much from the outside, so little from the inside. From the point of view of accurate description, there is only one side of the wire fence that can be considered the right side. From other points of view, the matter can be said to be reversed. The first time I saw Ruhleben, it was already dusk. There was six inches of snow upon the ground, and several degrees of frost. The soles of my boots were worn away from walking up and down the cell. I reckoned I had altogether walked 1730 miles up and down those eleven feet. I walked with my socked feet upon the ice and snow. It was very cold. After we had passed along a long brick wall, and had been admitted at a door half-way along, I found myself in a square. In the centre of the square was an electric standard with an arc light which flickered. Beneath this arc light walked up and down hundreds of dark couples. They walked energetically, and seemed to have some object in doing so. I learnt later that it was in order to keep warm. I was taken away to fill up my name on a slip, and for the policeman to hand over my money. I was given a receipt for the greater part of it, and was handed over about thirty marks in cash. There was a large map in the office, and for the first time since October I saw where the line was on the Western front. The last news that I had had, was just before I got over the frontier. Then the great retreat of the Germans from the Marne to the Aisne was in full swing. Of this, the German public heard nothing, but that their "right wing had slightly altered its position backwards"—"am strategische gründe,"[1] and then, much later, it was noticed that the daily reports contained mention of places that had been captured in the great advance. Gradually, the idea filtered through to the mind of the German public that they had retreated. The map with its flags and pins absorbed me immediately; I had not seen anything like it for more than four months.

Then a soldier took me. We went down alleys, through doors. Everywhere there were people. The place was crowded with them. We arrived at a tiny office, where somebody, after having been wakened up, gave me a white shaving bowl with *K.G.* on it, and a blanket that was at the same time diaphanous and wet. He then took me to what he called my barrack. I did not notice the outside in the dark, but the interior was a long concrete-floored passage, with a couple of electric lights. On each side were huge sliding doors. In this passage were a collection of unshaven individuals, wrapped up in vast rugs, overcoats, sweaters, mufflers, Norwegian ski-ing caps, all stamping vast iron-hoofed feet upon the ground. A great noise of chatter filled the air. I felt rather dazed by it all. Somebody came up to me and remarked he was the "captain" of the barrack, and he supposed I had better sleep upstairs. There was no room in a

---

[1] For reasons of strategy.

box downstairs, and little in the loft. However, I must manage as best I could. Everybody, frightfully keen to hear what anybody from what they were good enough to term the outside, had to say, crowded round and cross-examined me, fed me with bread, which was plentiful in those days, and stuffed sausage, jam and cake down my throat. I found speech difficult, and kept reversing all my words. It took a few days to get rid of this. I was the last packet of news from England—somewhat delayed in arrival. What were the people like at home? Were things as black as they were painted? "My dear sir," I was forced to reply, "I haven't seen the paint yet. The last I saw of England was——," etc.

I went outside into the snow, and up a staircase outside. I sat on a straw sack on the floor, and so did everyone. I lived for months in that place. It was impossible to stand upright in it, and at one spot the snow came gently through the roof. It was here I slept. The atmosphere was as thick as cheese; the whole place stank, and you could take the air, and cut it into chunks, throw it about and stamp on it, and yet it seemed about the same viscidity as mud. Nobody took their clothes off, or, at best, changed into others. We were so closely packed that it was impossible to put one's arms above one's head. The light went out, and an hour later there was silence. I could not sleep. The singularly inharmonic method of snoring that reigned supreme made the whole loft vibrate with these exgurgitory sounds. It was intensely cold. There was no air. I reckoned that there was one half square inch of window space per man, and my own particular half square inch was eighteen feet away and round the corner. The air was very thick. This particular loft had a wood floor, and the vast chunks of snow that were carried up by the wooden clogs that everyone wore, had made the wood soft with damp. Humanity, when compressed, stinks abominably, and this wet that pervaded everything made matters worse. It got into the straw sacks, and either the straw or the canvas had been used before; the past purpose must have been distinctly aromatic. These lofts in which we slept were the gables of the stables. Large beams ran in all directions, supporting the roof, which sloped to within two feet of the floor.

In this loft there were two hundred people in four rows; two back to back in the centre, and one on each side. The people on the side, if tall, were unable to stand upright. To anybody awake at that time, the scene was extraordinary; one light, that was left burning in case of fire, showed it up. The floor could not be seen for huddled forms that covered it. The atmosphere was thick and misty, but through it could be seen an avenue of clothing and personal belongings hanging from the low roof and beams, fading away into darkness in the far distance. Here an overcoat looked like a man hanging by the neck, relieved by the whiteness of a pair of pants hanging by one leg. Here, one man had put on all his spare clothing, and a cadaverous face projected out of the top of what appeared to be a diver's suit. Numbers wore Norwegian ski-ing caps, like polar explorers, and nothing but frozen tips of rubicund noses projected from out the woollen oval. Some, on the other hand, had scattered their spare clothing, if they had any, underneath or over themselves, and shirts in great sprawling embraces hid many a poor shiverer. Occasionally a word or so of conversation drifted up from the other end, and all night long the doors at the end banged, with people going out to the latrines, and every time great flakes of wind-borne snow would rush in, and swirl about, finally settling down evanescent and wet on some huddled form. So close were we all that there was hardly any gangway, and heads and feet got kicked and trodden on, and curse and prayer, like the serpentine wanderings of sparks in soot, accompanied any riser making his way to the door. "Damn your bloody soul, why the hell can't you look where you're going to?" or, "Oh, for God's sake don't knock *all* my rugs off. You might at least put them on again when you have done so," or, "Look here, I'm wet enough as it is: if anybody else bloody well opens the door to go out again tonight, I'll go and bag their places while they are gone. I'll risk the lice. At any rate, they'll keep me warm." Coughs of every sort went to make up that chorus of noise. Occasionally a great rumble comes from the deepest valleys of a man's lungs, and myriads of little yapping sore throats rasp away in attempts to attain a status satisfactory, and all the while the discordant hum of vibrating tonsils forms a background to every other noise. Nearly two hundred forms, just animate, lay there, each with two square yards in which to live, to eat, to sleep.

No one will ever know how much hope, how much despair, how much determination, how much suffering was hid in each of those two hundred huddled heaps. For a time I lay awake, thinking, to the tune of my neighbour's breathing, of the new order of things in which I found myself, but gradually as a feeling of thankfulness that at last the worst was over, and that I had got out of that ghastly solitary, spread over me, I fell into a doze, only interrupted by occasional urgent messages form my feet that they were aching with cold, and would I kindly pull the coat over them. I was awakened by a sore throat, a general noise of people getting up, and a soldier walking round, with a searching eye for lie-a-sacks. Dim forms were shedding clothing of all sorts, and I, perforce, rose up and joined them in the process. I was doubtful as to where one washed, or, in fact, whether one washed at all, until I saw semi-nude forms with basins going past in the gloom. I joined them after charitably being asked to share a basin and sponge, and rushed outside into the snow, and round into the concrete passage below, where two taps did duty for the whole three hundred and sixty of us. We formed a great queue of semi-naked forms, towels hanging round our necks, shivering almost harmonically, dragging one heavily clogged foot after the other over the rough-laid concrete, as we gradually approached towards the slowly running tap. It would have formed an interesting subject for sociological investigation, to have noted the percentage of those who washed and those who didn't, and to have classified, analysed and accounted for the latter. It was a task that, as I neared the tap, I intended to perform, and as I left the latter, with my basin slopping the water all over me, I decided had no value.

Dressing finished, I followed the general run of affairs as best I could. People, I noticed, were taking their white enamelled bowls, and rushing out at the door at the end. I did the same. Outside on the ladder staircase the blackness of the sky was changing to dark blue, and the stars were beginning to fade. The snow on the ground made the scene look bright. On one side, as far as I could see, was a collection of long, low-roofed buildings, their roofs covered with snow that overhung their edges and dripped great icicles to the white ground below. The red-bricked walls, the small windows, the snow, and muffled figures moving to and from without the noise of footsteps, all contrived to give the scene the air of one of Carmen Sylva's stories of the old German villages on Christmas day in the mountains. This impression lasted me a minute, and I was swept away into the crowd below. "Form up in fours; form up in fours" was the repetitive formula with which people were consoling themselves, in a manner like that of lugubrious church wardens. By a process of accretion, the little square block gradually took up the form of a vast rectangle of humanity. To give any sympathetic description of that crowd is a thing I defy anybody to do. Let it be said, however, that to a lunatic just released from solitary, or a man of sanity just interned there, these vast crowds, which could be seen dotted about various parts of the grounds, appeared like a cross between a London crowd of unemployed and a gang of criminals en route for Siberia. The resemblance to both was striking, for, not only were they formed up in the same manner as the latter, but they were dressed in the manner of the former. The whole mass swayed from on foot to another, so that their heads, viewed from above, appeared like the crests of choppy waves. The movement suggested the boredom habitual in those listening to a speech for the hundredth time, and, at the same time, a desire in those who are cold and are not allowed to move from the spot on which they stand, to become warm; as indeed was the case. "Antreten—line up, line up in fours," would run the moaning litany, with occasionally an emphatic shout, as someone lined up in fives. "Oh, see, there's the blokeoo arrived larst nite from prisn. Myat don't ee arf look a sod! Thai putim in prisn fer sixteen bloody weeks, all by is bloody self, yes thai did, you arsk im if thai didn't. Ee woz in England for the fust two months of war, and then ee comes hover ere." "Ee didn't!" "Ee did." "Well, ee must be a bloody fool."—"Oh, good morning; I hear you arrived last night. Allow me to introduce myself."—"Hullo, mate, find this a bit different from chokey. Little bit of all right, ain't it, six in a box down-stairs, and a couple of hundred in the lofts. Bit cold last night, wasn't it?"—"I heer dthat you haf djust arrived here. They dreat uz Engliz very bat here in Chermany. I vos two veeks in——"Still we stayed there, and the soldier who had wakened us wandered up and down. For full half an hour we stood thus, shivering with the cold, hands in pockets, and shoulders hunched, and ears stinging with the biting of the wind. Then, suddenly, our soldier said something, and we went off at a shambling trot, which should have been a walk, but owing to the prevalent desire to get warm, relapsed into the above method of progression. We followed in and out of long barracks like our own, until we emerged into the square with the electric standard which I had seen the night before. We crossed this, and, proceeding through a gate, we rushed up a small and iced incline. On our left were three colossal blank red-brick walls. We halted. Again for half an hour that ghastly wait. One by one we went in through a small door, and a continual stream of individuals, intent on bowls full of some black substance, issued forth in a gentle cloud of steam from out another. As best we could we carried that coffee—for it was coffee—back to our bar-racks. Here and there one would meet a brown sunken splash in the snow, showing where a slop had come out over the edge of somebody's basin. We climbed the stairs, and sank on to our mattresses. As I lapped the coffee in thank-fulness, the day was spreading over the sky, and the last star was receding into space.

CHAPTER XI

THE CITY OF FUTILITY

THE CHARM THAT I FOUND in Ruhleben was purely relative, and it soon wore off. It is difficult, perhaps, for those whose tongues are only limited by what they have to say, to understand how intense the pleasure of mere intercourse can be. I would lie back on my sack, and just listen to people borrowing spoons from each other, or cursing each other for mutual coffee slopping. A universal shout of laughter would make me warm with delight, and a continual cry to someone to shut up or to make peregrinations Hellwards would make me pause over every delectable syllable. Less, however, was the pleasure I took in the physical surroundings. It was my first morning there. I did nothing. I lay huddled on my sack of straw, vainly hoping that I might one day know again the meaning of the term warmth. But it was not long before a cry arose from the far-off depths of the loft, of "Everyone outside please, outside please," and I had to make a supreme effort to move my wretched carcase. I was still grasping my coffee bowl in a frantic attempt to get heat, long since flown. I stumbled numbly up and towards the door, and after passing two hurrying people with brooms, went out into the snow.

It was very cold. There was a wind that cut. I found the scene of the night before repeated. Hundreds—thousands— of forms, black against the snow, were moving like ants in every direction. Couples passed you with an air of purpose, and before the eye had followed them to the end another with an air even more purposeful had compelled its withdrawal, and led it in a direction more attractive. What was everybody doing? I must find out, and get some to do as well. I was standing thus—like a lighthouse amid the scurrying of the waves, when two dimly remembered figures suddenly laughed, and clasped me by the hand. We shook hands vibratingly, but I had to confess that though their faces were vaguely familiar to me, I could not remember their names. They were two old Cambridge friends, people I had never expected to see again, and whom I had completely forgotten. I found a large Cambridge and Oxford colony and we were all very merry. I still had nothing but a thin summer suit, and a perfectly diaphanous shirt, the soles of my boots were worn away, and I had worn my one collar for sixteen weeks. My friends swept me away and clad me from head to foot in clothes that made my body glow with warmth. All of them gave me something, and I should have attained the proportions of a prima donna had I accepted everything in which they tried to wrap me up.

It is very soon along the scale of exigency that the sacred rights of property are limited and by common consent. In a place such as this was, the right of ownership is decided by a communal "Sittlichkeit,"[1] and the strange point is that most people do not notice that there is any difference, and that the propertied seem just as happy with their limited

---

[1] Morality.

rights as they do with their rights absolute. My friends, and their friends, not merely clothed me, but fed me for the first few days, gave me stores and books, bored themselves with my company and left not a stone unturned to bring me back to life. For the first day they made it their amusement, but thenceforward it was their task, and no set of men ever did more, even when impelled by pleasure. It was not merely my friends. People I had never seen before were continually doing things for me, men whose purse was short and who had a limited amount of parcels sent them from home.

I went with one friend to fetch a parcel that had arrived for him and from which he was going to give me some supplies. First, in order to make certain that there was one for him, we went round to the "boiler house." This was a gawky species of agricultural boiler, with a chimney nearly as long, in proportion, as a growing boy's arms are to his body. Over the butt end, that is to say, over the fire-box, straddled a wooden protection that made a box for the person who stoked it. One side of this "boiler house" was plastered with notices.

"The Lancastrian Association will meet at three o'clock on Wednesday at the right-hand top corner of the third grand stand."

"Will all those who hail from Hull or York or Timbuctoo meet at the first grand stand at three o'clock on Monday. Mr. Timothy Tomkins has a letter from the Mayor to read."

"Does anybody wish to buy a really new pair of Russian officer's top boots, first-class leather. Barrack 1."

"Wanted a copy of Chaucer's *Canterbury Tales* and Pitman's *Ready Reckoner*. Barrack 6."

"Have YOU had YOUR pipe carved as a memento to take HOME to YOUR friends? You should. Tom Noddy of Barrack 8 will do it for you just top hole. Prices moderate: hours 10-1, and 2-4."

"R.D.S. (Ruhleben Dramatic Society) will give a representation of B. Shaw's *Androcles and the Lion*. Book your seats NOW. Stalls 60 pf. Dress Circle 30 pf. Gallery 10 pf. Standing room."

"Wanted a teacher in Sanskrit. Apply Barrack 2, loft."
"Mr. ——— is willing to give lessons in Hindustani. Loft, Barrack 3."

"The orchestra will practise every day and all day. Signed— —, Conductor, Captain's box, Barrack 6."

And then finally came the parcels list, with about six hundred names, after consulting which we moved off, in the same directions as from where "breakfast" had been obtained. The blank wall I had noticed was the back of a grand stand, over the other side of which was a race-course, where we were not allowed to go. There was a slope of ground between the wire fence with its perambulating sentry and the stand, and up and down this there walked still more hundreds of people. It was like a bank holiday crowd on Hampstead Heath, only more crowd and less holiday and no Heath. There were three stands, all in a row, and at the butt end of one we found four colossal queues that seemed to stretch away into wonderland. My friend calmly went to the tail end of one of these and began standing there patiently, like a wet fowl in the rain. It seemed a terrible but inevitable thing to do. Even though I was now supplied with boots I found standing in the snow too great a strain, so I left my friend swaying lugubriously from side to side and making an occasional step forward when the figure in front, who was pendulating in the same manner, permitted. In three-quarters of an hour I returned, and found him still occupying himself in the same way. "Heavens," I remarked, "when are you going to get your parcel?"

"Oh," he replied, "I'm not waiting for my parcel. This is for the slip; that is the parcel line there."

"Slip, what slip?"

"You are given a slip that has been filled in by the sender in London and you present that, you see, at that window there, and the parcel is given out at that window over there to the left."

"Oh," I replied, "I see. I'll come back in an hour." I did. He was just getting his parcel. It was now nearly time to line up for lunch. When we had lined up for lunch, which consisted of a potage with occasional cubic centimetres of hairy pork floating moodily between globules of grease, and had lined up to wash out our bowls, at one of the taps the barracks provided, I lined up in order to buy some stores at the canteen. In those days it was possible to buy rolls and loaves of bread, but this was before K.B. (Kriegsbrot)[1] had been made compulsory. After an hour or so spent in the snow in this amusing fashion, I went on to what was termed

---

[1] "War bread," which substituted much of its wheat with rye and potato flour.–P.C.

William Whitely's to buy a few articles of clothing, such as handkerchiefs, gloves, etc., also soap, a mirror, etc. After lining up for only ten minutes, I found they were out of stock. Whiteley's was kept by the villain of a contractor who at the request, but not under the supervision, of the camp military authorities, supplied diverse substances to the camp as food, with the result that though he fed, he also pocketed thousands. He was eventually kicked out on attempting to make millions. He was given 6d. a day per head to feed us, and he spent about $1^1/2$d. He went by the euphemism of "Greaser." I hear he has now retired from business, and has a beautiful flat in the Potsdamer Strasse, Charlottenburg. With my purchases from the canteen, such as Oxo cubes, I lined up once more to get some hot water from the spout, which supplied us with the condensed water of the hot-water pipes.

CHAPTER XII

THE INNER MEANING OF ORGANISATION

CHRISTMAS TIME WAS the commencement of a change in the lot of the prisoners. When I arrived in February matters were considerably improved. The commanders of the camp and the barracks were soldiers. To the latter we gave money, to the former grovelling respect. The result was that though, for instance, drink was strictly forbidden, one night a whole barrack of three hundred to four hundred people was absolutely drunk. One man, with whom I used to go to breakfast occasionally, would always ask me what liqueur I would take. For a considerable time all newspapers were forbidden, and *Vorwärts* or any English paper was strictly forbidden at all times. Nevertheless, I always saw all the German newspapers, including *Vorwärts* and Maximilian Harden's paper the *Zukunft*. We had the number that was suppressed by the Government in the spring. We had a regular subscription to *The Times*, and never a week went by without our seeing that, or some other English paper. One method would be detected by the military and we would discover another. Some men used to earn their living by getting hold of English papers and letting them out at sixpence to one shilling per hour. It resulted in there being a species of club of persons who subscribed to obtain news.

It was the irony of fate that I obtained far more news of what was going on in Germany when I was in Ruhleben than I did when I was free. I remember one story from an Englishman, a friend of Mr. Brand Whitlock's, who had been in Brussels at its surrender. Count von Arnim, who was in command of that particular German army, was entering Brussels, and Burgomeister Max went in company of an official from the American Embassy to arrange the terms and particulars of surrender. It was necessary that Count von Arnim should see the American Minister, and he accordingly drove up to the Legation and inquired for Mr. Whitlock. Mrs. Whitlock received him, and said it was a matter of great regret to her, but the General could not see Mr. Whitlock at that moment, for the latter was in his bath. "But I must," said the General, "it is necessary." The upshot was that General von Arnim, his neck and back very rigid and stiff, his breast scintillating with decorations in expectation of a state entry, was received by Mr. Whitlock, who was swathed in a bath towel dressing gown.

In order to satisfy a German creditor, or to look after German interests, prisoners were often given a holiday for a few days or a week, and, until it was put a stop to, it was the great thing to get your wife, or your mother-in-law if she be German, to sue you for half a sovereign. Anybody who had left a bill unpaid was careful to make no response to letters from the creditor until a summons arrived, when a petition for a holiday was promptly made. Now, unfortunately, a species of local court sits in the camp itself, to take evidence. But until it was suppressed, this was a most prolific source of news.

In this way we heard of the great amount of damage done to the Badische Anilin Fabrik by French airmen. We heard that this was one of the main manufactories of the asphyxiating gas and bombs. The buildings were so close together that when one of them was hit by a bomb and, by reason of its contents, took fire, it was impossible to prevent it spreading to the rest.

I could never obtain confirmation, but one rumour that became very persistent was at the time of the Austro-Italian negotiations; Germany was obviously putting great pressure upon her ally to make concessions, and Austria, it was said, in return for these was asking for compensation from Germany. The small quadrilateral of territory around Glatz that projects into Austrian territory was to be conceded to the latter, if that should be the wish of the majority of the inhabitants, and a vote was actually in the process of being taken when Italy declared war.

Nearly all German soldiers are venal as long as there is no risk attached to the service involved, and *The Times* is freely sold in Berlin. The complete disorganisation that reigned in the camp for the first few months made it possible to do almost anything. There are roughly four classes of German officers. There is the first-class man at the front, who really is first-class, the first-class man at the base, who is likewise; there is the second-class man at both; and then the aristocratic and incompetent, who is reserved for such establishments as prisoners' internment camps, with the result that Ruhleben was, and to a certain extent is, one welter of disorganization. The military camps are in a category apart, for it was only natural that war would produce military prisoners, but the civilian prisoners were not expected. No plans were made for them. There were practically no rules that defined their treatment. Had there but been a Zivilgefangenverwaltung[1] before war broke out, quarters as neat as a chess-board would in all probability have welcomed the arrested civilians, instead of stables from which the horse-dung had not been swept. We should have had officials whose duties, defined with precision, would have left us no hope of attaining power ourselves. Fortunately it was not so. Graf Schwerin, who was responsible for the camp, was a benign old gentleman, member of a famous family. He managed the external affairs of the camp, and when I last saw Ruhleben he interfered but little with the internal arrangements. Once when General von Kessel, whose son is a prisoner in England, the Commandant of Berlin, a great personal friend of the Kaiser's, sent an order that no smoking was to be allowed in the camp, Graf Shwerin ignored the order that lay on his desk, and telephoned to head-quarters to say that he would resign if it was insisted upon. Baron von Taube, a wealthy Prussian squire of some sixty summers, is the "camp commandant." He was a man of extraordinary incompetence and temper. He is neither strict nor lax for any length of time, and flies from one policy to another with a speed in proportion to the intensity with which he followed the last. His obstinacy is usually irrational and his actions are generally likewise. He can never be relied upon to remember his orders of yesterday, and seems to think that the camp officials have done wrong if they obey what he eventually believes to be stupid. One of the mercantile seamen there interned once expressed himself rather freely as to the nature of Prussians. The Baron went round the camp, and, to one after the other of the four-

---

[1] Civilian Prisoners' Management Board.

teen barracks, to the tune of many resounding thwacks upon his decorated breast, screamed, "It is not we who are the bloody ones: it is not we who lusted for war and brought it about. I give it you back: you are the bloody ones." Later the Professor of English at the University of Berlin, who was interned there, with several others went and explained to him the meaning and derivation of the English term "bloody."

There was a vast amount of amusement to be got out of the camp authorities. On one occasion, when there had appeared in the *Lokal Anzeiger* a couple of lines rumouring the possiblity of an exchange of civilian prisoners, Ober Leutnant von Amlungsen, who is in private life a small wine merchant, and in military life a bully, rushed up to the kitchens and told them to be careful not to order in too much food.

There were various other officials. Graf Bismarck, nephew of the great Prince, was set to see that the parcels coming into an English internment camp contained no drink. The Graf's duties at the parcel-post office not being of a particularly onerous nature, gave him ample time for intercourse in the camp, and he made many friends among the prisoners. General von Bohëm, the Ober Kommandant in the Marken, on a surprise inspection of the camp, remarked in a loud tone of reproach to the Graf, with all his brother officers present, that it was well known at the Kommandantur that whenever the prisoners wished to know anything, So-and-so, a particular friend of the Graf's, asked him and was immediately satisfied. Soon after this incident, the nephew of the Great Prince was removed from his position of supervising the opening of parcels. His place was taken by Graf Hochberg, a well-known friend of the

Crown Prince.

The one figure that interested me more than any other was that of Rittmeister von Brocken. I never spoke to him, or had anything directly to do with him, but I made a close study of his habits. He was responsible for the guarding of the camp and the behaviour of the guards. I do not know whether he still holds his position.

Perhaps the most remarkable feature of the camp is the body of captains about whom so much has been heard. When the camp was first constituted as an English camp in the early days of November, each batch of prisoners, as it arrived from various towns, was put into one of the stables that are called barracks. For practical purposes, the barrack soldiers asked for an interpreter, and chose anybody with a fluent knowledge of the language. After a short time had elapsed, the camp authorities, finding it necessary to communicate with the prisoners, did so directly through these interpreters. Later they were appointed Captains. Very rarely they were elected by the barrack they were supposed to represent, but even in these cases, Baron von Taube would appear and remark that the inhabitants of the barrack wished So-and-so to be captain; did not they? and the barrack generally acquiesced in a somnolent fashion. Graf Schwerin was opposed to all forms of parliamentary government. Usually the captains were entirely appointed by the Baron or the Graf. However, after numerous disagreements, the captains have secured the right to co-opt any new members of their body that necessity may call for. The rise of this body has been very analogous to the rise of the Commons in England. True, the magnificent power of withholding supplies is not theirs, but in view of the fact that the Authorities in charge there are perfectly incapable of managing the camp themselves, the captains are generally able to obtain their desires by a judicious use of the threat to resign and throw the entire machinery of the camp in a state of wreckage into the hands of these aristocratic incompetents. The German soldier cannot, above all things, endure being laughed at, and though his dignity does not permit a threat of that nature to be used frequently, nevertheless, as time proceeds and the machinery for looking after the affairs of 4500 people becomes more complicated and fearsome looking, so does the power of this body of "captains" become greater and more secure. The military are, more and more, in a peculiarly insidious manner, being forced, to their utter mystification, into the position of a purely permissive body, and it may be of some interest to see where they eventually terminate their career.

Camp Commander Baron Taube with his staff in the
English Civilian Camp at Ruhleben.

CHAPTER XIII

THE CATEGORICAL IMPERATIVE

I SPENT THE FIRST ten days of my stay at Ruhleben trying to find out if there was any chance of obtaining an exchange. At the end of that time I not only came to the conclusion that there was none, but also suddenly got taken ill with double pneumonia. Prison, though it had its drawbacks, was warm. Ruhleben was never so, with the result that one day I found breathing difficult, that my head was hot, and that I had no appetite. That evening the loft captain, a most charming fellow, who spent the whole of his life there in altruism, sent for the one man in camp who boasted any medical knowledge. The long and the short of the whole matter was that for days I lingered at death's door in the atmosphere of that loft. My friends nursed me day and night, taking it by turns to sit up with me. They got hold of the most wonderful things to feed me on, and Heaven only knows where they got them in that place. They had been continually urging the military doctor to come and see me, but he always replied that I could come and see him between nine and ten any morning that I cared to. One evening, thinking that they would not be able to keep me alive throughout the night, my friends got hold of the commander of the camp, and induced him to telephone to the doctor, who was in Berlin on pleasure, to return at once. He did so. The doctor's mentality as regards myself when he arrived was, Is he dead? If not, why not? He gave me two aspirins, and remarked that I was too ill to be moved, remarking a little later in the week that I wasn't ill enough. He had me both ways. He never came to see me again. I survived, as perhaps the reader who peruses this may surmise, but my heart was badly strained as a result.

During the weeks that followed, I spent day and night upon my back. I was too weak to do a thing for myself, and, during all that, with all the long days and nights, to get through, I became more and more of a day dreamer. The misery and the futility of such a life took hold of me, driving me to the determination to do something—anything— to avoid more of it. My friends did everything that human kindness and superhuman ingenuity could devise, but nevertheless I felt stifled, crushed, comatose. The determination to escape arose without any thought as to how it was to be done. It was not for several days that I even began to consider any plans. I had seen so little of the camp that I was untrammeled by any awe of the authorities. I knew that if I should eventually take on the idea and stick to it long enough and hard enough I must pull through. I knew it. I felt positive. I at once began dreaming of my home-coming—of what I would do in England, of how pleased and above all how surprised my people would be to see me. I pictured Easter at home, though later I had to admit that this was somewhat hasty. I dreamt of England, waking and sleeping, until one day, I suddenly discovered that, though I had determined to escape, I had forgotten to think of how it was to be done. In those days, it was in February, I thought that getting out of the camp would present no difficulties, for, as far as I had seen, there was but one row of sentries, and they appeared very sleepy and slack, and I thought that I had already detected a flaw in the arrangements of their beats; but my doubt lay in what should be done when this was accomplished. The Dutch frontier I threw over as being the obvious place where they would look for me. Besides, I had heard how the Swiss frontier was guarded, and I imagined that the Dutch was looked after in the same fashion. In order to prevent the Alsatians travelling backwards and forwards into Switzerland with military information, an electrified barbed wire, guarded on each side by a fence, was erected right up to the Austrian frontier. This arrangement was doubled. Armed sentries walked up and down in between the two. Ordinary barbed-wire fences divided it up into squares. All fences had bells attached to them. Now arrangements such as these are extremely difficult to deal with, because while they are being treated in a proper manner, a sentry appears, and the game is up, within sight of neutral territory. The Danish frontier was impossible, for it was now impossible to get across the Kiel Canal without papers, and it was harder to creep through the sentries guarding it than to cross the frontier further on. The one frontier that I thought would not be guarded at all, or extremely laxly, was the Austrian frontier. True, I was not yet out of the wood even when in Bohemia, but I was possessed of the feeling, "Oh, let's get out of Prussia, and then we'll be all right." It may possibly have been irrational, for it was the result of fear. I knew that I was risking prison and solitary for the rest of the war once more, but I was driven forward, in spite of myself, by a lust for the fresh clean air of freedom. Whatever risk, whatever dangers should crop up, I knew that I should never be able to resist this instinct of self-preservation. My scheme, just vaguely drawn up, was, after having got out of the camp to go through Berlin, which was but ten miles distant, to walk by night along the road to Dresden, and thence to go up into the mountains above Schandau and go very gingerly across the frontier into the Bohemian woods. There, I thought, organisation of all sorts would be less stringent, and I could take the train for a few miles every day without fear of being asked for passports. A fortnight's judicious training should bring me round to within forty miles of the Swiss frontier. It might be safe to go into Innsbruck. As for food, I must carefully accumulate the meat tablets and strips that were reaching me from home. I spent pleasant hours in counting out the lozenges, and granting that, if so many boxes reached me per week, when I could make a start. It was just a little over a hundred miles to Dresden, which I reckoned was a big enough town for me to be lost in, and in which therefore I might buy food as if I were a resident. I saw at once that I must only be seen in towns that were so big that I could get "lost" in them, or so small and so remote that there would be no search for me. I could not believe that the co-operation between the Austrian and German officialdom was so close that my description would be telegraphed into Austria. In those days I attached great importance to the efficacy of the hue and cry that would follow my departure, and I was desperately keen to avoid the obvious. They would naturally send off telegrams to guard all the frontiers of the Empire extra sharply, but it seemed improbable that they would consider the Austrian frontier as being a frontier at all, "within the meaning of the act."

They would naturally argue, I would say to myself as I tossed from one side to the other on my straw sack, that it would be out of the frying-pan into the fire, and it is this very thought that will prove my safeguard. I began concocting stories, to account for my not being in the army, to tell peasants in lonely huts in the Bohemian woods when I wanted to buy food. I got hold of a map of Europe, and, as far as I could measure the distance, it appeared to be about five hundred miles right round to the Swiss and Italian frontiers, and six weeks, I thought, would see me in one or the other. I began collecting information about the passes above Schandau. I spent three weeks in this manner, and I fixed the 2nd of April for the start, should I be strong enough by then. Then, suddenly, I got wind of the fact that a couple of army corps had been sent south into the Tyrol, and I had to give up the scheme. This was the failure of the first plan.

I was so pleased with the idea of leaving Germany by the Austrian frontier that I was very loath to surrender it, and besides, my investigations as to the Schandau neighbourhood were progressing very satisfactorily. I had found somebody who knew the district well, and I professed a general interest in mountaineering which made him talk. I carried the names which he mentioned in my head until I was able to write them in Greek characters on the floor. It was, of course, impossible to ask him outright for a description, as it would have indicated at once what I was thinking of, and, though there are many men whom one can trust not to betray one, there are but few whom one can trust not to open their mouths. When men have nothing to do all day long but talk, they become so garrulous that it becomes impossible to keep even the slightest and least important bit of news locked up inside one. It would be an interesting experiment to put a cabinet minister in such circumstances. Many a good story would probably be told, under the seal of the strictest secrecy and absolute confidence. Comparative statistics as to the number of people who did not mention his revelations in their diaries would be an instructive help in the foundation of the science of prison psychology. I can remember now the odd method I used to employ to get this man to talk about the Säxische Schweiz (the "Saxon Switzerland"). He had been a great deal in America, and was very fond of telling stories about "Potash and Perlmutter." From these I used to get him on to American railways and their comforts or discomforts, thence to the American mountains, e.g. the Rockies; from that a comparison with European mountains was easy, including, of course, the Säxische Schweiz. I had to spend four or five days before the whole transition could be effected, as from Potash to Shandau is a far cry. Nevertheless, with patience, it was accomplished, and every day my knowledge of the place grew greater. As the Swiss and Italian frontier seemed hopeless, I quite seriously considered the Roumanian. True, it was about a thousand miles away, but I attached such importance to the fact that any official whose duty it was to find me, would not think of this route, that I favoured the idea, unless other difficulties should arise and throw it over. I pictured myself once over the Austrian frontier as taking the train daily for about thirty miles, and then walking carefully by night to a village a little further along the line, and training once more, until by this process I should be within a hundred kilometres of the frontier, when it might be advisable to walk.

Then I met my friend Falk.

I can remember the afternoon quite distinctly, that I had gone up to "William Whiteley's" to buy a 2d. mirror, and an extremely handsome boy with merry blue eyes that seemed capable of greater suffering than most, after staring at me aggressively for some moments, remarked, "Oh—er, excuse me, but—er—aren't you the fool—er, I mean, aren't you the fellow who was in England for the first two months of the war, and who came over here? Well, come along and have some tea. Barrack 3, Box 8." It was later on in the evening that, after pushing back the heavy sliding door, I found myself sitting in the dark with six others around a table that I could have surrounded with my arms. Tea made from the condensed water of hot-water pipes was served out with great liberality, and, to the munching of Genoa cake, I told all that I could of England. There was silence for a time, and then they plied me eagerly with questions, till every detail that I could remember was theirs to keep and think over. "We must apologise," they remarked, "but the Camp Pessimist is not here yet; he'll be in soon," and it was not long before the door rolled back, and a compact little figure came in, and quietly climbed up on to his bed. "Give me some tea, Molly, and introduce me." The introduction is performed with great éclat, neither of us realising all that it would mean for the future. I found that Falk's pessimism consisted in the main of the power of summing up pros and cons in a masterly fashion, and that this annoyed associates who preferred an aggressive optimism, and what seemed to me an insane belief in the inevitable fact of our muddling through somehow. On one subject, however, he was a terrible pessimist. He would go round the whole camp, announcing with a certain lugubrious satisfaction that Napoleon kept his civil prisoners for eleven years. He was rich in historical precedent and could quote any historian on all subjects. He was worse than a pessimist. He was an amateur strategist. In fact, he might be called a real strategist, for he had been a military man and had succeeded in hiding the fact. He had been an inspector in the old volunteers, and, on their death in 1905, he had entered the Political Service of Nigeria, where he had quickly risen to the position of District Commissioner. He had been over for a few weeks of his holiday in Germany, when war broke out. He was arrested before war was declared when on his way back to England, and had been placed in solitary for more than a fortnight. He was eventually released, though not until he had been through the ordeal of being told by a court martial that he would remain there for the rest of the war. We discussed the prospects of the war till we were all red in the face, and raw in the throat, and then we all dispersed through banging doors into the darkness.

I saw but little of my friend for some time, when, now that I was convalescent and able to get about somewhat, I met him wandering up and down the slope outside the three grand-stands that was called the sea parade. He was very gloomy about something. Afterwards, I became so used to his pessimism that I have now forgotten what the subject was that had driven away a temporary wave of normality. My own gloom was even blacker and more abysmal than his, but I soon found my oppression was inculcating positive optimism in him. Thenceforward, I always knew what to do when he was taken very bad with the blues. He would never admit that this was the proper pessimism, but misnamed it cynicism.

It is difficult to propose such a thing as escape. We were both very careful, and approached the matter delicately. It was quite a month before I dared even get on to the subject. We grew into the habit of meeting daily. At first we used to discuss the state of affairs prevailing outside; and then, when wandering round the camp, I pointed to a part of the fence and remarked, "That's not very carefully guarded, is it? Look how slack that sentry is. One ought to be able to get out there if One was fairly sharp about it." "Yes," Falk would reply, "but what would One do when One had got out? You could take the tram into Berlin, and go on the bust for the night, and what then? You'd find it harder getting back, wouldn't you?" "Yes, I suppose One would," I replied, and let the subject drop for the time. But the next day, when we were strolling about together, competitive in pessimism, I edged for the same point once more. "I say," I murmured, "that fellow *is* slack, isn't he? One ought to be able to do it quite easily there." "Yes, my good fellow, that's all very well, but what would you do when you had got out of the camp?" my friend replied rather testily, in a for-God's-sake-don't-tempt-me sort of voice. "Oh, One could always have a shot at it," I remarked. "A shot—a shot at what? Now, suppose—for the sake of argument—that you had got out of the camp, and had reached Berlin, what would you do then? For all one knows it is necessary to have a passport or a *polizei ausweis*[1] in order to take a ticket." I said nothing more that day. Within a week I had found a man who had been released for a short space of time to Wiesbaden, to bury his grandmother or his aunt. For half an hour I induced him to talk on the state of affairs outside. I questioned his ability to judge, remarking that he had only travelled by train there and back, and of course, when he had had his pass examined, the rest of the carriage would naturally have known that he was English, and would have shut up like oysters. "Passport,

[1] Certificate from the police.

my dear man, passport, why you're talking through your hat. You don't have to have any pass; why, I tell you I listened to dozens of conversations, and in all I heard the same thing. They all said that Germany—etc. etc."

The next day again found Falk and myself near that part of the fence. We had been discussing Imperialism, when I remarked suddenly, "You don't need passports to travel."

"Sure?"

"Yes, positive."

"How did you get hold of that?"

I told him.

We went on talking of what One would do, and what One wouldn't do, until one night, when I had been urging a scheme with particular fervour, I changed it to "I."

"I should do this, Teddy," I remarked, and as I told him my scheme I threw all the invitation I could into the tone of it. I was glad to notice that he made no sign of having observed the change. I was convinced by now that, though I might get out of the camp and into Berlin by myself, I should find it almost impossible to pull off the rest of the scheme alone. My friend had an almost unrivalled knowledge of affairs German, and spoke the language perfectly. His experiences as a Commissioner in West Africa, where he had to administer a province the size of Prussia, gave him powers of resource and agility of mind that was simply remarkable. Above all he had extraordinary powers of judgment, though, as I have remarked, he was abysmally prone to pessimism. I was desperately keen to present the mere idea of escape in a favourable light. I recalled his own opinion of our chances of release or exchange. I presented his own quotation of Napoleon's precedent. I acknowledged that, though I did not think we should remain there as long as eleven years, yet I was convinced that we should be there for three. "And imagine," I would continue, "spending three years of one's life in this place."

His God—he would moaningly reply.

The next morning we were both a little shy. Both of us had experienced the effect of waking up in daylight immediately conscious of our last night's plan as a new factor in life, and neither of us was quite certain as to whether in the other this feeling had not overswamped the determination of the preceding evening, and made it appear as the product enthusiasm and imagination. Falk, I think, rather wanted to test the strength of his conviction, so he put up numerous objections to the scheme, and, by admitting that he had been foolish the night before, offered me a way out, should I feel bound otherwise to go forward. His objections, however, soon collapsed, and we spent a morning, now that the ground was really cleared for action, that left nothing to be desired. It was perfect. We spent an hour constructing and demolishing ways and means, and speculating on what we would do when home. This always annoyed my friend, who regarded Providence as specially prone to temptation. He refused to allow the topic, he said, till we were safe in a neutral land. But I poured sweet alluring phrases into his ear, and mersed myself in the joy of being back home once more. Then we would return to the plans, and home would take its proper place in the scene, and the prospect of the future become once more correct, sane and judicial.

We surveyed the area of operations anew. The Swiss frontier and the Dutch frontier, it was mutually agreed, were both impossible, the one rendered so by the fear of the Alsatians, and the other of the Belgians trying for a place continually further and further north, until that part of it was reached where the military would be on the look-out for spies watching their naval bases, such as Wilhelmshaven. The main railway arteries run not far from the Dutch frontier, and it would be only in conformity with the general plan if it was watched for persons who attempted to pass it in order to spy upon the movement of troops. *Ergo* Dutch and Swiss frontiers were out of the question. The Austrian, as I have said, was seemingly *hors de combat*, and my friend did not share my optimism as regards the lack of vigilance in Bohemia and the Tyrol, let alone the frontiers.

Then, for the next two months we concentrated on a plan at which I had long been working. Somewhere to the north was now the only possible route. The Schleswig frontier was impossible now, by reason of the Canal, which was guarded by sixty thousand soldiers with unceasing vigilance. There was no other land frontier. The sea was all that remained.

From Warnemunde in Mecklenburg to Gjedser on the Danish isle of Falster is twenty-five miles. The sea is fairly shut in, though strong currents run east and west. In summer there are often slight mists hanging over the water. My idea was that even if we could not risk taking the train, the 140 miles that lay between us and the coast could be walked by night. I knew the Danish and Swedish parts of the Baltic, also the island of Rugen. In all these the pine trees come down to within a few feet of the water's edge. Once on the coast, after spending the day in hiding in these woods, we would creep down into the water and swim out to any small boat that we had sighted in daylight. We would hoist her anchor and her sails, silently move out into the night, to arrive at Gjedser in time for breakfast the next morning. I knew of a charming little inn there where they not only give you good meat and bread, but also rögröd[1] porridge if there be any left over from Sunday. Yes, the northern route was most decidedly the best.

But that plan broke down. It was the third that we had been forced to abandon. Every day we would go through the newspapers, looking for indications as to the precautions taken outside. One day I came across the fatal announcement, among a whole series of rules for the Ostseebäder, that all the small bathing piers (that jut out into the Baltic from all its shores, whether Danish, Swedish, Finn, or German) were to be stripped of their planking. It was obvious that if precautions such as these were being taken in fear of a Russian landing, then among them was sure to be a rule that all boats were to be pulled up on shore. And even though the Baltic is tideless and therefore they need only be pulled up a little on the beach, the risk of arriving at the coast and being unable to move about without disturbing the occasional sentry there was certain to be along the coast, was too great to make the idea tenable any longer. For a few days we examined the chances of success of smuggling ourselves on board the Warnemunde-Gjedser ferry, or on a neutral vessel at Rostock.

Then I decided finally that if we could not steal a boat there, that we must take a boat with us.

---

[1] This may be a mispelling by Pyke of the Danish term rö(d)gröd med flöde, a sort of porridge with cream.—P.C.

CHAPTER XIV

WHICH WAY? WHAT MEANS?

IT IS A MATTER of almost vital importance that if you are going to turn your hand to out-manoeuvring or out-cheating a person or persons, you should have very definite ideas as to their mentality. Most things are a battle of mentalities, though one mentality is often static. Contrary to the usual opinion, if a prisoner is devoting all his powers, all the time to the creation of a means of exit from his cage, unless his captor is devoting all his powers all the time to keeping him in, the chances are all on the side of the prisoner, always provided that he can retain all his mental powers and will go forward from one discouragement to another automatically as if by instinct. Solitary confinement and other products of civilisation may rob him of all powers (and it may have that purpose in view) of observation, of originating, of application, of judgment, of decision, and then he can do nothing but let the steam-roller squash him out flat. It is unlikely, however, that he will succeed, even should he retain all his powers, unless he be conscious to the uttermost of the nature of the mentality opposing him. A study of the mind that made the prison bars will lead him to search for faults where the bars themselves reveal nothing but strength. The Prussians appreciate this fact, and make use of it. They assiduously collect any personal data they can about the personal qualities and even habits of the commanders opposing them.

I repeated to myself countless times, "Well, if we can't get boats there, we must take boats with us," without quite grasping the meaning of the phrase. I saw plainly that it was a logical conclusion, and that was all. But how to take boats with us? Then I saw it—portable canoes.

There are no means of getting from Berlin to the Baltic by water, with the exception of the Oder, that are not complicated and enormously long. There is no route by which one can go all the way by river, and avoid the barren banks of canals. But within fifty miles of the coast from the lake of Gustrow, for instance, there are rivers that would take you out through Demnin behind the sandy, pine-clad peninsula of Zingst. At some points the sandy, pine-clad Zingst is but one thousand yards or so across. And it is twenty-four miles from one of these points in Zingst to that inn in Gjedser I spoke of, where not only is the bread and meat good, but where they give you rögröd (and cream) if there be any left over from Sunday.

If you, reader, were to see three young men dressed appropriately in white flannels, paddling about on the Upper Thames, say near Reading, would you take them for escaped prisoners from the Isle of Man? The young men in white, by the very fact of their being in white, with their hair cut according to the national custom, and their shoes, their ties, their socks all perfectly English, would rush in and take possession of your mentality, and it would need to be something very positive to eradicate the subconscious effect of the whiteness of their trousers, and the correctness of their shoes, shirts, and ties. Nay, if someone were to rush round the corner shouting that there were three escaped Germans in the neighbourhood, do you think it improbable that, as you are not as young as you were, you would turn to these young men, and suggest that they should use their legs to join the chase of those despicable Huns. And imagine something more, say the dishevelled and portly constable, who charges round the corner as if chased by a leopard, were to say, "Have you seen a brace of Huns?" or even to ask for merely one Hun, would your suspicions rest on two or one of those three young fellows, their paddles resting while they gaze surprisedly at the constable and the water rocking them gently up and down as it goes lap, lap, lapping against the sides of their canoes? And as you wish them good morning you would remark that you hope the brutes will be caught, and one or other of the three young men will answer that he hopes so too, and so you will part, you to go your way, they to go theirs. This is what I mean, if I haven't made myself clear, by occupying the mentality of the average citizen. On an expedition of this sort I saw that the more of us there were the better, and that as long as we could rely on not being missed for some time, anything up to a dozen would be appropriate. The idea was to be a "Gesangverein" or singers' union. We should have a flag on the foremost canoe, with the union badge on it. The Lusitania Verein was a good suggestion, and the hymn of hate could have formed our main support. We decided to ask another man[1] to come with us, and I approached him delicately. At first he roared with laughter at the idea, as Falk had done. He had an

---

[1] Wallace Ellison, a businessman caught in Germany at the start of the war. He was the captain of Barrack 13.—*P.C.*

uncomfortable feeling it was too mad. Finally, however, we all three agreed upon it. It was now the beginning of June. Then the canoe scheme broke down.

When I had originally produced the idea my friend Falk merely remarked that he supposed I should grow older one day, a truth which, from the way he stated it, I started to combat, though later I admitted that it was a possibility that might eventuate unless my career got cut short suddenly. About the same date, a camp magazine had been started and the printer had sent specimens of his art. With my usual luck, one of these samples had been a yachting paper, and therein was an advertisement for portable canoes. The whole difficulty was solved. I promised to lay thank-offerings before the goddess of fortune, for she was indeed favouring me. My friend was, however, even in the face of this obvious indication from heaven, still perfectly adamant, and it was not until two weeks later that I had overcome his objections to the scheme. And by that time the printer's sample had been thrown away, and no amount of searching in the rubbish heap was any good. We no longer had the address of a portable-canoe maker. We were undone.

I was perfectly convinced that it was almost impossible to outdo the Prussian. The only hope lay in outwitting him. As time wore on, and plan after plan broke down, I became more firmly convinced than ever that something utterly and hopelessly mad and impossible was necessary. For all things sane and possible the Prussians have taken precautions. *Ergo* nothing was left but the mad and the impossible. I paid more and more attention to the psychological side of the business. My determination not to stay in Ruhleben was fast approaching white heat. Night and day I lived in a perfect fever of desire for home. I tried to give myself another type of mind. I tried to induce in myself the type of the super-logical or the super-intuitive. I became certain that the Gaboriau-Conan-Doyle-Sherlock-Holmes[1] sort was no good at all. The Germans are up to all that sort of game: Holmes being merely a somewhat bourgeois Englishman, with a taste for Watson, might work quite well where the two extremes of logicality and intuition work side by side, where he would never be understood in his mixture of sweet simplicity and cocaine; but he would perish miserably in Prussia, and would be outdone all along the line, from his comfortable dressing-gown to the Italian violin. But his great rival I at once perceived would utterly bewilder and dumbfound the Prussian. The immoral and decadent Frenchman, besides producing his "seventy-fives," had reproduced himself in the figure of one Arsene Lupin. The great charm about Arsene is you never know quite who or where he is. It is just the opposite with Holmes. All you have to do to find our friend Holmes is to say, "Whom do I least expect him to be disguised as? Why, this horrible filthy old creature, of course, who is just going to ask our dear Watson to spare him a copper, as it's very cold to-night." But Arsene hardly ever is so puerile, so banal as to think of the idea of disguising himself. He simply becomes two people at once. He is simply the prince of criminals and the chief of police at the same time, and nobody can say whether the chief of police took to crime, or the prince of crooks to guarding the property of the public. And the whole thing works beautifully. Without following any specific adventure of Arsene's, I tried to change my mentality

---

[1] Pyke, a tremendous reader of detective fiction, is referring in the section that follows to Émile Gaboriau (1832-1873), who ranks with Poe and Doyle as an early influence on the genre.—P.C.

into his. I tried to stop myself thinking in any other way, even about small trifles, than he would. I was very serious. We were near the middle of June.

Then I evolved the boiler scheme. The great disadvantage of getting out of a country inside something is that the authorities are liable to open it, and it was therefore necessary to get hold of something that gave the appearance of there being no room inside. The scheme was as follows. Either Falk or myself was to get out of the camp one night—in those days we considered it quite an easy matter—and to go into Berlin. There, whichever one of us it be, was to go to a house agent and, with terrific swagger, to hire a yard. Thence he was to proceed to a well-known maker of agricultural boilers, and, after a decorous amount of inquiry and bargaining, to buy a boiler as airily as possible. (I found out later that they cost about £400.) This accomplished, the firm were to be instructed to send it to the yard. He would then telephone to a firm of engineers and ask them to send a skilled workman along, who would be instructed to knock all the tubes out, in order to clean the inside of the boiler, and to cut them up two or three feet from each end. The artisan would then be dismissed, or told that there would be nothing doing for several days, and meanwhile another would be summoned to restore the butt ends of the tubes. This one would be told that we were on the verge of a great discovery for the more effective generation of asphyxiating gas, and that for this the centre part of the tubes were worse than unnecessary—in fact, they got in the way—and as he saw, only those opposite the man-hole would be preserved. All this nicely disposed of, the best firm of Berlin expediteurs were to be instructed to fetch the result and dispatch it to a well-known firm in Copenhagen. Finally we were to bribe one of the seamen in the camp to come into Berlin with us and screw down the man-hole. Food and water for a fortnight we should take with us. There would be heaps of air, as we should be breathing through the amputated tubes into the smoke-box and up the chimney. But the scheme broke down. Fortunately, in the camp there was an *Encyclopaedia Britannica*, though it was of colossal age. In this I read all I could about boiler construction, and found to my horror that "the better type of boiler has copper tubes." The export of copper from Germany is, of course, forbidden. The whole question now resolved itself into whether or not the customs officer at Rostock, knowing that better-class boilers have copper tubes, would, after ten months of war duty, undo the manhole and peer into it with an electric light. The risk was too great, and the money difficulty was insurmountable.

Suddenly we found that it was impossible to get out of the camp. There was but one row of sentries, and it had been quite easy to find several places where one might climb over the fence without being caught. But we discovered that, in addition to these, there was a caretaker who looked after the race-course and all its buildings in peace time, that he still continued his work, and that he came on duty at seven o'clock in the evening, and left it at six in the morning. He was a tiny little creature, and somewhat decrepit, but he went about with a dog who seemed very much alive. I had studied the sentries, and made an absolute science of sentry-going. I could look at my watch at any moment of the day and know the exact spot where every sentry ought to be. I had taken averages; I had drawn graphs. I could have taken an examination in the subject, and have come out with a first-class. But the little man with the dog upset all this, for he had no definite beat, but wandered about all over the palace, poking about with his stick, egging his dog on to investigate anything suspicious, and altogether making himself thoroughly objectionable to prisoners who intended to escape.

I saw no way of getting round the fact that it was impossible to tell at any moment where he might be; so I was driven to the conclusion that if we couldn't escape at night, we must do so during the day.

CHAPTER XV
FREE

ABOUT ONE O'CLOCK on the morning of the 10th of July, in a small hole on the top of a rise of ground in the Charlottenburg woods, my friend Falk and myself were lying shivering and whispering. All round us were the pine trees. They rose from out a low mist that was just perceptible in the darkness. Above, the stars were shining brightly. The only noises were occasional and distant. We tried to sleep and could not. We were both excited at what had just been accomplished. The great scheme for getting out of the camp in broad daylight had worked almost without a hitch.

It will be a long time before I forget the moment when I said to my friend, "Well, I've made up my mind for to-morrow afternoon. I'll come back in half an hour and see if you've made up yours. I shall go in any case." And then again that next afternoon, when, as arranged, I met him opposite the grand-stand. Both of us were very serious-looking. "You are quite certain of the whole thing?" he whispered. "Perfectly," I answered, with an awful fear that after all my observations and calculations might have a slip in them somewhere. "Is it time yet?" he asked, and I looked at my wrist watch, which showed six o'clock. There was half an hour to wait before we were to begin. We waited. It was a half-hour of life that was well worth spending. I felt artificially calm about the whole matter, and more of a captive than ever. The sun was getting low, though it would be another two hours before it set. Something very terrible was going to happen to me, and quite soon. In half an hour's time Falk and I would either be shaking in the grip of a couple of German soldiers, or the possibility of a totally new life without horizon would extend before us. It was like waiting for reincarnation, with the alternative of death.

At last the minute hand pointed to the half-hour, and we began to move. Now I felt a natural calm, as if I was observing the workings of fate through a telescope. Till we arrived in our tiny sand-pit, where we now lay, with the sweat cooling upon us, I genuinely enjoyed myself. The whole scheme worked most beautifully, and it is a matter of the keenest regret, the regret of an artificer at having to conceal his handiwork from the sight of men, that both my friend and myself have agreed that, until the German military authorities have discovered how we accomplished it, or circumstances render discretion nugatory, the secret shall not pass our lips.[1] Suffice

---

[1] After the war, Pyke was able to reveal their plan. Roll was called in the morning but not in the evening, on the sensible assumption that prisoners escape at night. One fleeing during the day (were such a thing possible) would not be noticed missing. But only nighttime provided sufficient cover to escape—hence, nighttime security around the barracks was vigilant. Therefore, the trick was to leave under cover of the night, *but not from the barracks*. There was a small equipment shed at one side of the camp, and Pyke noticed that the afternoon glare through a window was so bright that one couldn't really see inside, even though guards went through the motions of opening the door and looking in. So he and Falk spent the afternoon hidden in almost plain sight in the shed. After dark they crept out of the shed and escaped through the camp's perimeter.—P.C.

to say, however, that it was a combination of the idea of the Trojan horse—we always referred to it in our talks as the wooden horse, in case of being overheard—and the effect of light coming over a solid. If the sun be setting over the top of a mountain the mountain will appear like a black mass, and nothing similar colour, unless it appear on the sky-line, is visible. This was something of the same kind. In case, dear reader, notwithstanding this obscurantism, your brain has leapt to the puzzling out of the secret during the last few lines, let me save you any further trouble by saying that the scheme depends on a number of local circumstances that I have omitted.

The plan was supremely obvious, and it still remains there for any one of the denizens of Ruhleben whom it stares in the face, and who cares to take the risk. It can be employed any day of the week, and there is nothing in it that depends on chance. It is a "dead cert." Should this book ever, by some means or other, come into the hands of a Ruhlebenite, I beg him for the sake of all that he holds dear in life, to use meticulous care should he employ this means of exit and ingress. It is too precious a thing to spoil by care-lessness. You will be quite safe, oh former companion mine, for I have heard that the military are on a track that is hope-lessly wrong...one, in fact, which makes me consider it an insult that they should think me so stupid, for all that they have done is to put sentries at every thirty yards, a sheer piece of buffoonery that makes no difference whatever.

We were outside the cordon of sentries and the wire fence. It was half-past ten, and the last reflection of light had disappeared from the sky. Everything was quiet. We were hiding in a small copse of trees at one end of the camp. It had been inadvisable to go any further before it was quite dark, because of the number of soldiers and officers who were always returning from here. Not many yards away was the end of the sentries' beat, and we could see the blaze of the electric lights that dotted the wire fence at every few yards all round the camp. We began to move off. During the preceding ten days, there had been five attempts to escape, which had considerably disturbed the military, and, though they had set in motion a rumour that the whole camp was shortly going to be exchanged, they had also taken the precaution of putting out at various positions around the camp fifteen extra sentries, and try how I might, I had been unable to find out where they had been placed. I behaved extremely caddishly to my friend at this point—not to mention scores of others, for I carefully concealed this little bit of news from him. He was married, and had two small children, and I knew that, had I told him, he would have refused to come, rightly remarking that for their sake he must not do anything rash. He was as jubilant at our success as a confirmed pessimist could be, but I had to suppress this recalcitrant tendency in him. Modern sentry-going, as the reader probably knows, does not follow the old system in its entirety. With the possible exception of one cordon, the guards do not walk up and down, but stand perfectly still, their bayonets ready, listening. This I surmised would be the case here. I had evolved, during the course of two months, two especial methods of crawling, one which I called the crab-crawl, by which one could proceed in one direction, and yet keep one's eyes fixed on a sentry in any other. The second method, which I dubbed the caterpillar method, had sheer speed, combined with a modicum of invisibility, for its purpose, and depended on lifting the knee at a certain point in the movement. I had practised these openly in sight of the whole camp, and had said they were part of a system for the curing of weak heart of a Dr. Sörgersund, a Dane, whom I invented.

Following the first method, we moved off very slowly, our boots hanging from our mouths. It will be a long time before I forget the precise taste of boot blacking. I know that as we went slowly on, the boot would sometimes drag against something on the ground, and I would feel that the blacking was getting mixed with the sweat which was streaming down my face. It was vitally important that we should arrive clean, for I had heard of a Russian officer who after escaping had been caught, merely because he appeared somewhat dishevelled. Suddenly I saw a light. "The little man with the dog," I whispered. "Run!" We risked the fifteen extra sentries and, changing quickly to the caterpillar method, simply raced on hands and knees as fast as we could go. It was a false alarm. We spent close on two hours crawling about two hundred yards. We had purposely described a large semicircle, and had now arrived in line with the racecourse. Near here we knew there was the road we were aiming at. As we were about to get up on our feet a huge fence of wire-netting surmounted by the usual barbed wire arose out of the darkness. For five minutes we lay perfectly flat, not even whispering, both waiting to see if it was guarded by a sentry. Then we got up, and my friend climbed on to my back, and, putting his feet into the interstices of the wire, climbed over. The agony of listening to the noise he made, and his pitiable appeals to me, when my turn came, not to rattle the wire so frightfully, is one of those hundred incidents that can be left to the imagination. Ten paces further on was another of these fences. This time, any idea of waiting was out of the question, for if there was a sentry anywhere, his obvious beat or position would be on the road made by these two. This time my friend was on my back and over in a minute, and after handing him our boots over, I followed him as quickly as I could. Now we moved along fast, almost at a run, for the sentry, if there was one, was now behind us, and, though we were showing up dangerously against the sky-line, we stood a fair chance if he tried to shoot us through the fence. We had hardly got out of earshot when we found ourselves opposite another fence, the biggest we had yet come across. It was something worse than tall. Instead of having the barbed wire on the top of the poles, the former was carried on brackets that leant backwards at an angle of forty-five degrees. As I was the taller, my friend got on to my back, and, with a great deal of difficulty, got over, and dropped softly to the other side. It was then my turn. I pulled myself to the top, but could not get my leg over the barbed wire. I had to let go. The result of my previous illness had been to leave my heart very weak, and, when after pausing a moment for breath, I tried again, once more I got to the top, and once more I could not manage that barbed wire so cunningly placed. Try how I would to prevent them, my arms unbent, and I slipped to the ground, sick and dizzy, my heart fluttering in my ears. For a time I just leant against the wire, my fingers grasping it, ready to make another effort when I felt a little bit stronger. The night was very dark, a cold wind was blowing gently against my streaming face, and my friend was softly beseeching me from the other side to make another effort. If a sentry were to come along at this point I could do nothing. I could neither try to climb again nor could I run fast enough to avoid his hitting me for an absolute certainty. I should whisper to Falk to go, as he could do no good by stopping. The sentry would come on shouting, and putting up his gun. He might fire at me, and say afterwards that I resisted, or attempted to run. If not, he would take me roughly by the arm, and drag me triumphantly to the Wache.[1] I should spent the night in the cells, and the next day I should be taken to prison, and then all over again would begin that terrible period of walking up and down, doing nothing, no longer even hoping——

I had got to the top; I had got over the strand of wire that leant back; I had not an ounce of strength left. I could do no more. I just held on, balancing myself. Below me was my friend; he was looking up at me and his face was singularly intense, and I saw that the boot blacking had left a smudge below his mouth. He must be saying something, for his lips were moving. It was odd, for I could hear nothing. Then suddenly his face grew larger, and I began to dream. I felt him catch me, and in a moment I had come to. I felt him shake my hand, and I did my best to give him an answering shake, as we stumbled on away from Ruhleben.

In a moment or two we struck the canal that we had been able to see from the camp, and followed very warily along the tow-path. There was a light in the distance, but it was impossible to judge how far away it was. Before we had time to retreat, we were in its range. We could see two forms, and a long thin-nosed motor boat. "River police boat," I whispered. "What's to be done?" "Nothing," he replied. "Go straight past them, and wish them good night. Say it's rather late, isn't it?" Boldly, with fear in our hearts, we stepped out, and it was not until we had spoken, expecting in answer the cry of "Halt, wer Sind sie," that we found

---

[1] Guard room.

155

they were two old gentlemen waiting for a ferry from the other side, and that the motor boat was anchored and covered over. This was our first encounter with inhabitants of the outside world.

And now in a slight hollow in the earth I was lying, with my hands behind my head, smiling contemplatively to myself, and watching the stars fade away in the face of the first glimmering of the first day.

CHAPTER XVI

BERLIN ONCE MORE

WE COULD HARDLY keep from laughing as we walked down the Spandauer Strasse through Charlottenburg. There were not many people about, which enhanced the novelty of the experience. Whenever we passed anyone I would say to Falk, "And what happened then?" and he would reply, "Oh, she got furiously angry and——" His German was a great deal better than mine, so that if perchance it became necessary to continue the story of the lady's rage, he could do so without any fear, while there was always the chance that sooner or later I might make a grammatical slip, especially if I should try to decorate the story. Henceforward Falk took charge of the expedition for those occasions on which consultation was impossible. The getting out of the camp had been my speciality, and he had worked microscopically, with what turned out to be brilliant success, at all possibilities that might arise after that.

We had gone about a couple of miles and there were yet five or six more to go before we should reach the centre of Berlin, so we stopped at a tram halt, and boarded the next tram. It was full inside, and we stood on the platform at the rear, where there were already a crowd of people. The face of one of them—a soldier—seemed curiously familiar to me, and I was suppressing the idea as fancy, when I looked down at his shoulder strap. It was bright yellow, and had E on it in red letters, which stood for the Elisabeth regiment. I don't know whether he saw anything in me, or whether he was attracted by my gaze, but for a few moments we stared each other up and down. Then he turned to his friend and began chatting again as to what he was going to do with his twenty-four hours' leave. I regret to say he was a very bad man. I felt very whimsical, and itched to tell my friend, who was tucked away behind a fat Hausfrau, that we had two of our own soldiers from the camp on board the tram. They did not belong to his barrack, or to mine, so the chances of our being recognised after that preliminary stare had been survived were not very great. We got off not far from the Stettiner Bahnhof, the station where I had arrived in Berlin ten months before, and walked into the best restaurant we could find in the neighbourhood. Though we had mutually scraped and wiped off as much dirt as possible, we still looked slightly dishevelled, and it was necessary to account for this. We were therefore engineers, and had been up all night, and as we walked into the restaurant, which was practically deserted, Falk remarked that he would certainly send in his resignation to the chief if he had to stay up all night much more, and where could we wash our hands please, preliminary to breakfast? And then we would have breakfast. Omelette? Good, omelette for two then. Not even in the solitude of the lavatory did we depart from our rôles, and when at table we still kept it up.

That breakfast was a break in life. Everything looked different, even when it was but half consumed, and I felt perplexed that I saw nothing in the faces of others to show that they too recognised the change that had come over the world. It was our first real meal for the greater part of a year; our first meal with a table-cloth. This was our first waiter for that time. One wanted to hit him on the shirt front to see if he was real. The first time we had seen trams, women, umbrellas. When I saw a top hat, I had an overpowering desire to roar with laughter, and to point it out to my friend. I nudged him as we walked, but I could see by the firm set of his mouth and the fact that he kept his eyes steadfastly averted that he too had seen it.

During the breakfast we had casually asked for a time-table, and had looked up trains for the well-known tourist resort of Goslar, in the Harz mountains. The train left at midday from the Potsdamer Bahnhof. My wily friend in selecting this route and this station had been guided by the fact that it was not the direct route for the frontier, and that the probability was that neither the station nor the train would be watched.

There still remained a couple of hours in which to do the shopping we had planned. We had both of us accumulated money during the preceding months. It had not been a dif-ficult thing to do, for it was only necessary to send in an application for a fur coat and the sum was handed out to you from your account. I sent in applications for a whole wardrobe, including, I think, seven fur coats. Of course, a great deal of this had gone in the ordinary expenses of liv-ing, and in my having a suit especially made for this occa-sion, but we had about £5 a-piece—every penny of which we used, and which represented about the cost of an ordi-nary ticket in peace time. We had gone over what we intended to buy very carefully, and our first purchase was a couple of umbrellas, great big fat things, that looked as if a boy of twelve had tried to roll them, in deference to parental orders, and had done it as badly as possible on purpose. We then walked with an air of great business towards Wertheim, in the Leipziger Strasse, Berlin's great store. I was so interested in the place that I clean forgot I was an Englishman escaping from prison, who by this time was probably badly wanted by the police. We wandered from one department to another, buying vigorously. Our purchases, considered all together, might possibly have aroused suspicion, but nobody ever saw the whole list. First came rücksacks. It was great fun turning a whole section over and over, changing one's mind time after time, with the result that when we were finished with this one purchase, the assistant had room for nothing else in her head but the desire to get rid of us. We further exasperated her by spending a long time while over the choice of a collapsible cooker. I was a expert on these, and it immediately recalled to mind many a joyful hour spent in meticulously choosing a kit, preparatory to long expeditions in Norway or France. Finally we chose a beautiful aluminium arrangement with two saucepans, a frying-pan, a wind screen, that used solid lumps of spirit, folded up flat, and cost under half a sovereign. Nothing like it has yet appeared in England. And as I write this, that collapsible saucepan, its shining aluminium surface blackened and dented with use, occupies the place of honour on my mantelpiece. I look over my shoulder and regard it with brotherly fondness, and hope that both of us may yet survive to make many an expedition more in company. Though we had not yet attempted the most important purchase of all, we next proceeded to an aluminium water-bottle covered with felt. I remember distinctly that we paid

1s. 9d. for it, though I have been unable to buy the same thing in England for less than 7s. 6d. We wandered on to another department, and were tried on with Loden cloaks, great black things, whose only virtue lay in the fact that they rendered anyone who wore them perfectly shapeless. We bought them. For a time, everything went smoothly. We purchased clothes-brush, collapsible aluminium knife, spoon and fork, handkerchiefs, and electric flash lamp, and several vast slabs of chocolate. Then we ascended by the lift to the top storey, and for a "brother-in-law at the front" we purchased a luminous compass. This was vital—how vital we were yet to understand. But when we were paying the bill for the last-named, the cashier suddenly said, "Name and address, please?" Without the faintest hesitation my friend invented a name and culled an address from space. It was one of the many things for which we had not prepared, for we had both imagined that by the time it came to asking names and addresses, the game was up. I don't remember what name he gave, but the street was Lutzow Strasse, No. 14. I asked him later how it was that he had been so quick in bringing this out, and he told me that every town in Germany has a Lutzow Strasse. It was then that I remembered having passed a Lutzow Strasse in the town that morning, and realised that No. 14 could have been nothing else than a public swimming bath. Though the cashier's request for name and address made me jump, I noticed that her suspicions were in no way aroused after Falk had answered with such perfect aplomb. I had never observed till placed in these circumstances how infinitely more listless the women assistants are than the men. During the course of the whole expedition I always found that the women were not so suspicious as were the latter. The former were probably shockingly underpaid and overworked, and had energy for nothing more than a wish that the day might come to an end. With the exception of an elderly creature who sold us the Loden cloaks, I saw no male assistants, and it was the same among the customers. Indeed the whole of Berlin struck us both as being a city of the dead. Everywhere we saw women in black and men in uniform. There was but little traffic; even the trams did not seem so frequent. A fortnight later we were to have Amsterdam with which to compare it, at least so we prayed.

We had suddenly reversed our opinion as regards the Dutch frontier, partly because of necessity, and partly because we had heard of an English journalist who, while on the Dutch frontier, had suddenly found himself in Germany and had been arrested. He was supposed to be due at Ruhleben, but we had never heard of his arrival. His *faux pas* did not seem to indicate the existence of electrified barbed wire, though it was possible that the latter stood back a short way from the frontier, which might also have guards. Time would prove to us which it was.

As we passed out of Wertheim's, a man, who seemed to have nothing particular to do, stared at us keenly. It lasted but a moment, but it puzzled me. We were heavily laden with parcels and nothing could have looked more bourgeois; nevertheless, it wasn't a good omen. Of course, it might have been merely nerves, but I ought to have got over that by now. As we went across the Potsdamer Platz, I observed in the distance a remarkably familiar figure coming out of a café. "Look," I said to my friend, "there's von Taube; what a colossal joke. He doesn't know either of us from Adam." The figure turned away up a side street, and that was the last we saw of the commandant of Ruhleben.

There was still half an hour before our train went, so we went into the buffet, and after ordering a drink, began to unpack our parcels and put the things away in our rück-sacks. The cloaks we put over our arms. This unpacking was a mistake, as we both of us later agreed, for it made us slight-ly noticeable, and it was possible that the waiter might remember the two men who had left a cardboard box behind, and had tipped him for his trouble when he objected. Observing this, we had left the place as soon as possible. Falk bought the tickets, and he felt his guilt staring out of his eyes as he faced the scrutiny the booking clerk levelled at him.

We strolled on to the platform, and went and gazed at the products of the bookstall. Most of the books were of the expensive war-book type—something like this—and as I stood there hesitating which to buy, for the first time I recalled how ten months ago I had stood hesitating in just the same manner at the bookstall of King's Cross. I remem-bered how I had stood gazing numbly at wonderful books by Messrs. Hall Caine, William le Queux and Miss Marie Corelli, at pamphlets telling me why I was born in April, and how it was really all a mistake on my part, December being essentially the proper month in which to be born, and how it could all be rectified even yet, if I would but expend the sum of one penny. Mrs. Florence Barclay, I remembered distinctly, flourished there, and six shillings would have procured me thousands of words' worth of long drawn-out, passionate kissing. Mr. Nat Gould was to be found embraced on one side by Sir Walter Scott, and on the other by Mr. William de Morgan and an A.B.C. time-table. There had been pamphlets all about the White Slave Traffic, and next to them a book by Mrs. Humphrey Ward all about the

Church of England, and then a little volume, telling me how to cure myself if I be an unmitigated drunkard. It all came back to me, how I had hesitated at leaving pleasures such as these for the doubtful one of getting myself hanged or shot; how dark the station had seemed; how the bookstall had been the only light patch, and how untidy the bookstall clerk had seemed. I remembered how I had stared stupidly at the outside of one of Mrs. Florence Barclay's osculatory novels, and had then turned slowly away towards the train, with the feeling of a judgment passed upon me. And as I stood at the bookstall, exchanging an occasional comment in German with my friend, I reviewed the whole thing from the beginning to even a disastrous end, and I regretted nothing. Even in prison, with life at its blackest, I could look back and say, "And yet I regret me not." Neither then, nor even now do I know why this should be so, but I felt that, for a time at any rate, I had lived very intensely, and that this fact would remain for all time indelible.

And as the train pulled out of the Potsdamer Bahnhof and through the suburbs of Berlin, I knew that for this also, come what might, there could never be regrets. It also was indelible.

CHAPTER XVII

THE FIRST DAY

IT WAS FORTY HOURS since I had gone to bed, and soon after the train had passed through Potsdam, though I forced my eyes to follow the lines in the book I had bought, by no manner of means could I keep my attention fixed for more than a few words. With infinite labour I would commence a paragraph, and before I had finished the first sentence, the words I had read would form themselves into weird objects and notions, and I would wake up with a start to recommence the paragraph all over again. On each occasion I could see the alarm in my friend's face lest I should wake up suddenly and say something in English. At first, whenever he saw my eyelids fall and my head sink to one side or the other, he would press his umbrella hard on my foot. For a time he rested it there and at the first flicker of my eyelids he would lean his head and his hands on top of it, pressing with all his might. Finally I got so angry with this that he abandoned it, and whenever I dropped off, would jerk his head towards me, make some remark to the carriage at large, and I would wake up amidst their roar of laughter. When I smiled stupidly and sleepily in return, they would become more and more friendly, and I had an awful fear that kept me awake for a full twenty seconds, that a particularly buxom old woman was going to offer me her shoulder. After a time I gave up the unequal struggle and slipped gently into dreams, that rhymed with the bumping of the wheels at the rail joints.

We had settled on our respective rôles, and Falk expatiated on mine while I slept. He had become a compact little bourgeouis Jew—by name Blumenthal—and I was Herr Doktor—Herr Referendar—a kind of assistant under-magistrate. He would tell the carriage with great benignity how I had worked myself to death over my examinations, and how he was taking me away into the Harz for a rest. When anybody new got into the train, he would lean forward and tapping me on the knee to awaken me, would remark, "Well, Herr Doktor, how goes it with the heart?" "Ach, scheuslich," I would reply, and glide away into sleep once more. And thus without noticing it the new-comer was supplied with the reason for my not being in the army. My friend intimated that he was engaged in government contract, which cast a halo of respectability over him.

I awoke for good about an hour before we reached Goslar, and picking up the book that had dropped to the floor, I read until we arrived there at five o'clock. We were afraid lest we should be arrested as we left the station, for, though I had never worn the suit I had on until an hour before we escaped, I was uncertain as to how good a description had been wired to all the police stations. My friend had been in a horse-box in Ruhleben, and by stringing a curtain before his bed had induced the soldier and his box companions to think that he was behind it. I unfortunately had been in a large open barrack, and though for the last three months I had gone to bed every night with the blanket over my head, had risen every morning before the soldier came round and had kept out of my barrack all day, so that he might get used to never seeing me, I had but little hopes that the preparation would succeed.

I think that of the whole expedition this diurnal preparation was the hardest. Sometimes for weeks on end, when we had no plan for getting out of the camp, or no plan for getting over the frontier, it would need a sort of blind faith in everything coming all right in the end, the fanaticism of despair, to pull me from my warm straw-sack at six o'clock. I have been told since that my absence was discovered the same night, before really I was outside the premises, while we were still lying hid in the small coppice, before I had failed at that last terrible fence, while had a search been instituted, we could have been discovered with ease. And a few days before I write this, I hear that Falk's absence was discovered when, two days later, an order was suddenly received at Ruhleben that he was to be released into Germany. His small daughter of two years old had written to some princess, saying, "Please, I want my Dadda back," and the princess, being very Prussian and sentimental, had replied, "Oh, charmed."

Goslar is an old town lying in a valley at the foot of the Harz. It is chiefly remarkable for the fact that a German professor claims that neither Moses nor the Children of Israel came from Egypt, but that both originated in the Prussian town of Goslar. We passed through the old Market Place and up the main street, where we found a sausage shop. Thence we wandered to a common or garden grocer and bought chocolate, cheese, some maggi[1] soups, a small

---

[1] A Swiss firm known for making bouillon cubes.—*P.C.*

quantity of cocoa, and half a dozen eggs. We had intended to buy some wire clippers in Berlin, in case of meeting any barbed-wire obstacle at the frontier that we could not climb over, but we had forgotten to do so. After a consultation of three hastily whispered sentences, we decided that it was too suspicious at article to buy here, with rücksacks on our backs. Wandervögel[1] do not as a rule carry such implements.

Before we passed out of the town, we looked around for an inn, and finding one that looked exactly what we wanted, we entered. We ordered a most sumptuous meal—I shall never forget it—of three courses. Behind us were some young lieutenants, who were discussing something of overwhelming importance, to judge by their heads all grouped over the centre of the table. They did not trouble us much. Half-way through the meal the landlord who served us tried to persuade us to stay the night. Dearly as we should have loved to, we had to refuse him, for since June the police had to be informed within a few hours of the advent of any stranger in the house. He seemed lazily curious as to our movements, and we plied him with questions about the route over the Brocken which lay to the south-east. We informed him that we were going there for a walking-tour, and that we were starting that night as we had but a short holiday.

That night we went east. As the sun began to set we trudged out of the town, our rücksacks on our backs, our umbrellas as bulging as could be, and talking great mouthfuls of admiration. It amused us both vastly, as we trudged along in this fashion, to think that this was the home of a

---

[1] Hikers. Wandervögel ("birds of passage") was an early 20th century German youth movement focused on wilderness hikes and German folklore.—P.C.

man we had known in the camp. It was not long before we left this little town as we moved on towards the Rammelsberg. Numbers of small parties were coming down, and they all exchanged a cheery "good night" with us, as we toiled upwards and ever on. This was our first real night of freedom for ten months, and as we gazed through the woods at the pine-clad hills in the distance, we said nothing, for we had nothing to say, but stopped time after time to drink our fill of the view before us, and to realise yet more intensely the feeling of space and solitude. As the last glimmer from the sun disappeared we reached the top, and creeping in among the pines, we sought for a place in which to camp. We were more than 1500 feet above sea-level, and that night we shivered in the cold wind as we lay, trying to go to sleep.

The next morning, departing somewhat from the route we had told the inn-keeper, we descended to a point in the valley towards Berlin, and walked thence to the small village of Oker. Breakfasting here at the station inn, we asked for some eggs, but were told that there were none in the district, as they had all been bought up in order to supply the big towns.

On taking our tickets, we again had another panic, for the booking clerk had no tickets in stock for Bielefeld, the town for which we were making, and the fact that he had to make them out would be sure to stick in his memory, and provide a clue to the police. It was a Sunday, and the whole world was travelling. We had chosen it for that purpose. At times we were the only civilians in the carriage. We found the soldiers the least inquisitive of mortals. They were so anxious to talk about their own experiences that an occasional reference to Falk's "post" and my weak heart sufficed for our being in mufti.[1] There was nothing they didn't tell us. All that they knew was at our disposal, and we found them the pleasantest of companions on a long and tedious journey. We both of us felt perfectly German. We chatted with them about the English, and agreed with them that the latter, though brave, would never be able to stand up against our organisation. They showed us their puttees,[2] which they had adopted from the English, and vastly improved upon. When the conversation got somewhat slack, Falk would read out occasional paragraphs from the paper we had bought, and as he read out the reported fall of South-West Africa, I answered, "Reuterlügen." And I meant it. I felt that it was probably a lie, though I had previously been a Reuter correspondent myself. It was the next day, when we were walking across some fields, that we met a farmer who was directing the work of a couple of Russian prisoners. "Brutes, aren't they?" he laughed. "Rather," I responded, and I was surprised at the warmth and enthusiasm that I heard in my voice.

We changed several times during the day, and at the end we came to the superficial conclusion that the Germans still had another two million men they could put in the field. We based this on the mere impression that since we escaped from the camp we had seen about twice as many men in uniform as was usual in peace time. This would account for one million three hundred thousand, and to this we added seven hundred thousand maturing boys and old men who could still be squeezed out of the population. This was on July 11th.

---

[1] Civilian clothes.—*P.C.*

[2] Leggings, especially as used for hiking.—*P.C.*

We changed again at Löhne junction, and got into a compartment of the Cologne express that was almost full. They seemed inclined to question us, but Falk's remark that we had been for a holiday and were now returning "home" seemed to satisfy them. It was a little bit uncomfortable until we reached Bielefeld. Our great danger lay in the fact that my friend had been here so often before that he might be recognised by somebody at any moment. It was streaming hard; we had left one umbrella behind in the train, but holding the other over Falk, we strode out of the station as fast as discretion allowed. We walked into a small hotel my friend had been to but once a year before, and had what was to be our last meal. I remember noticing that it was remarkably cheap—two marks twenty-five for three or four courses. The reader might possibly get tired if I were to follow my inclinations and talk for two or three pages about the three meals we had after leaving Ruhleben; nevertheless, such is my inclination. They were red-letter days for us.

Hitherto on board the trains we had never been asked for papers, but it was impossible to go much further, for we knew that there was a lining of one hundred kilometres within the Imperial frontier in which passports were necessary. Bielefeld was about eighty miles from the frontier, and, being ignorant of the precise point where they first asked for papers, we had decided that it was not safe to do more than take a small local line. Following this plan, we went by tram to Brackwede and thence took the small local train to Dissen, a little health resort in the Teutoburger Wald. On getting out of the train, I made a frightful mistake. We had to cross over to the other side of the platform, and in the rush to get out of the rain, I got completely reversed in my ideas as to our direction, and on issuing forth from the station, I wanted to go to the left and Falk to the right. Each was firmly convinced that his direction was west, and for a time neither of us would go in the other, and we came near to separating. At last my friend, in his wisdom, came with me until we were out of sight, and then he whipped out the compass. Our heads both bent over the needle as it swung, and then I had to admit my stupidity and grovel lugubriously for my obstinacy.

It was nearly eight o'clock as we walked up into the hills in the other direction, and sat down solemnly in the woods, whilst the rain came down and drenched us for hour after hour. The light faded, and it became night.

CHAPTER XVIII
ACROSS NORTHERN GERMANY

BETWEEN ONE AND TWO O'CLOCK in the morning, huddled together though we were, with the umbrella over as much of us as it would cover, the cold and the rain became unendurable. We were under the thickest part we could find of the fir trees, and there was no room to walk about. We gradually stood up and swayed from one foot to another in our desperate attempts to get warm. As I put my hand into my pocket and felt that also to be clammy and wet, I realised that there was not a square inch of me that was dry. We remarked to each other innumerable times that this was fine weather for escaping, and how much longer was there before the sun rose? We still had a couple of eggs left, so we pulled the cooker out of the wet rücksacks that had served us for a pillow, and after cutting off a chunk or two of hard spirit, we fried those two eggs with meticulous care and vast solemnity. We were neither of us absolutely positive as to the science of egg-frying, but I was distinctly of the opinion that in order to prevent the egg sticking to the frying-pan, you must have some sort of greasing. When we had debated on this point, and the rain was becoming extra ferocious, we cut off a few slices of the sausage and vigorously rubbed them on the frying-pan. Had we known what was coming, we should not have been so rash. Those eggs were the quintessence of all that eggs should be.

We lay down again in the wet pine needles, and for the first time that night we slept.

The glimmer of a grey dawn woke both of us, and as I raised myself on my elbow, I observed a slight mist rising from off our sopping clothes. It was nearly five. We made our breakfast off one slice of sausage and one square of chocolate, and we both felt rather glum when it was finished. It was Falk, I think, who was the first to make the remark again that this was splendid weather for escaping; so few people would be out of doors. We squeezed as much water as possible out of our clothes and then got ready for the first day's walk. We had done with the train. Henceforward we were to rely on our legs and nothing else. In an absolutely direct line we were a little under seventy miles from the frontier. The route which the configuration of the land would force us to take was a little over eighty. We had got a school map that included the whole of Germany. My friend had given several lectures at Ruhleben to a class for commercial geography, and for this purpose it had been possible to get, without raising any suspicion, a map—good but distinctly small-scaled.

On this we plotted out the day's march. There were two parallel lines of low-lying hills running south-east and north-west, and our intention was to follow the southernmost one until it petered out near the Ems-Dortmund Canal, which we had to cross. Our fear was lest we should find ourselves nearing the frontier in country where it was impossible to find cover in which to hide during the day.

For one day we decided it was safe to walk in daylight and on the by-roads, but after that, when we were within fifty miles of the frontier, we must go only by night, and across country. With a strange feeling of novelty we set about to discover in which direction west lay, for being in the middle of the forest we had no idea. We followed the direction of the needle, but time after time the undergrowth became so thick that we had to go back and find another way. Our clothes were heavy and clung to us. Our boots squelched as we walked. The rain had even penetrated our hats, and they felt like bands of cold iron upon our foreheads, while they sent trickle after trickle rushing down our necks. At last we got out of the wood and skirted along the edge between it and some fields, where the parched crops were now lying beaten to the ground by the torrents that for the first time in ninety-two days had descended upon them.

In the distance we could see a road, and women and an occasional labourer going to work along it. We hastily concocted a conversation that must be transpiring at the moment a stranger appeared. Fritz, my friend was going to remark, ought to give us a good meal in return for this wetting we were enduring for his sake, and I was to reply that I hoped so at any rate, and that if he didn't I would never go near him again. We quickly decided that we were small farmers from the other side of Bielefeld, who had been staying at Dissen and were walking, since there was no train going in that direction, to Falk's son-in-law who lived near Ibbenburen. Fortunately we met nobody just then, though later we made a blunder that nearly landed us in prison. We had crossed the road we had seen on issuing from the wood, but had been forced to keep on another going at right angles to it. We met several people, and bade them a cheery good morning. The road was clear, and we were talking in English, very softly, it is true, nevertheless it was in English, when we heard a slight crackle behind us. We both jumped round, and at the same moment a boy of about ten put all the pressure he could on to his pedals, and dashed forward on his bicycle. He had been behind us for some seconds without our noticing it. As he disappeared in the distance, he looked back three times, as if trying to fix our faces in his memory. We reckoned out that he could not reach the next town for another half-hour, that it would then be another twenty minutes before anybody would take any active steps. We had fifty minutes, therefore, to spare. We let him go out of sight, and after giving him a minute or so to reappear if he wished to, we cut off up a lane to the right.

We soon got off the path and blundered on as fast as we could till we found a copse where we flung ourselves down in the depths of the dripping heather. Here we waited for a while, discussing what was the proper thing to do. This was an occurrence we had never though of before. Had that boy heard us talking English, or had he bicycled quietly along behind us in that fashion as some sort of game? I was rather inclined to this theory, after the new water from the heather had soaked through, and begun to cool me. I reminded Falk that I was the youngest, and therefore more able to under-stand infantile psychology. I urged that we should put our-selves in the place of the boy. "Suppose," I said, "you were living near here. Your father and elder brother are either at the war or in training. You find your mother is irritable and unable to appreciate the boredom in your life. School is just as usual. Nothing has happened since father's last letter. You bike to school every morning and along the same road. Everything is the same. You are pedalling very contemplatively when you espy a stranger. You creep up behind him as close as possible till he jumps round, and then you scud ahead for fear of his or her saying anything. You look round, and see what effect it has had upon them; if they are in a rage or not. Then you go on to the next person on the road, and see how near you can touch their coat with your front wheel, and so on till you find yourself quite close to school, with two minutes in which to get into form. Now which was this boy? Was he the boy detective or the boy puerile?"

With the help of the map, we tried to make out where we were, and for a long while we could come to no conclusion. About two thousand years before a Roman army under Varus had got itself completely tied up in these same hills and had been cut to pieces by Armenius and his Germans. The same fate, we said, seemed to be staring us in the face, for we could not make out which range we were on, or whether a few small hills we could see in the distance were to be considered as a range within the meaning of the map. Finally, we came to the decision that we were several miles out of our route; that we had describe a large semi-circle of about ten miles and must get back on to our proper range of hills as quickly as possible. It was nearly midday, and with the exception of an occasional rest, we had been on our feet for well over six hours, and on one square of chocolate and a slice of sausage. We had another slice of sausage, and a very small slice of cheese. As a criterion for the sausage we used the prongs of the fork, and henceforth we had one prong's worth of wurst per diem. The wurst was about an inch in diameter.

After a couple of hours of solid trudging, we sighted on the horizon a tower we had known to be somewhere in the neighbourhood. The district we were in is in peace time much frequented by tourists, whose pastime it is to climb to this tower on the top of the Dürenberg, and from there to gaze at the view before them, and then to go down and carve the name upon their sticks. We had a different though near-ly as important an object, in view; for the Dürenberg would enable us to fix our position and to see out over the land which we had to traverse that night.

We had had a lot of trouble after lunch with a soldier and his fiancée. We surmised she was his fiancée because of his osculatory manners. Whichever direction we went, ahead of us were always these two, and we had to lie down until we were quite certain they had disappeared. The rain had ceased, nevertheless the ground was still sopping. Before we had gone many yards further, looming in the dis-tance would be this affectionate couple, who, though we made desperate attempts to outflank them, continually extended their wing and effectually prevented it.

The transition from day to night marching necessitated either a rest of a day, or no rest at all. We decided to go straight ahead. At about seven we had suddenly, without meaning to, issued forth from the wood on to a main road. There was a woman on it, and further on an old man, and here again we both noticed the innocent stare of the woman and the suspicious examination of the man. We had to con-tinue along this high road until we could find a path branching off to the left, for to have come out of the wood on one side, and to have immediately dived into it on the other at a point where there was no path, would have sug-gested the idea of hiding to the least aggressive mind. It was very uncomfortable walking along that high road, for sup-posing that that boy had overheard us talking in English...

We cut off to the left at the first opportunity, and got far into the wood. It was not possible to go any further without coming out of it, so we decided to stay there till night began to fall. We slept for the greater part of an hour, and then made our supper off a thin slice of cheese and some cocoa. We then held a very serious examination of the food, at the same time reckoning out for how long it must last us. We had to admit that it would be needed for longer than we had imagined. Five days we had thought would be quite sufficient in which to cover the distance, but at the end of the first day we had to admit that at least seven would be necessary, and the food must be divided accordingly. This gave us so little per diem that we decided we must supplement it. We lay discussing ways and means, shivering and waiting for the darkness to descend.

In a little while we were creeping along the edge of the wood. Before us was a field, and beyond that was a field, beyond that there was darkness. That there were things growing in the field we could just perceive, but what they were we had to feel. I crept forward on hands and knees, for though it was preferable to be taken for a thief than an Englishman, I had little desire to be seen as either. I felt the leaves of the plants, and, deciding it to be potato, I scratched away at the earth till I felt the first one. With great trouble I got up about half a dozen of them, which we stuffed into our pockets as we went along. This was our first burglary. The difficulty of going quietly was enormous. We did everything we could, yet the silence of the night made our steps sound like the rustling of giants. We would walk ten paces, and then stop and listen, and then on once more. We were getting over a wall that lay in our route when the heavens rang with the furious barking of a dog, who in its efforts to get us dragged noisily at its chain. Exactly in which direction it lay was difficult to say, for we found our-selves in a farmyard, which echoed. Expecting that at every step a door would open, and an irate owner would issue forth, we crept on as fast as we possibly could, cursing the dog and all connected with it, until we came across a gate. We were over it in a flash, but finding ourselves between a wall and a cornfield, were bound to restrain ourselves for fear of the rustling. And all the while the dog continued its furious barking, but we could hear no door open. Numberless were the times in the succeeding days that this occurred. The harvest, we supposed, had made the inhabi-tants so tired that nobody was willing to leave his bed to come out into the damp to see why his dog barked. Once I actually trod on the toe of an animal that was asleep, and for the next hour, as we slowly crawled over the face of the earth, we could hear its dismal bark echoing in the distance.

We were unused to this slow cross-country going by night, but we both agreed it was safer not to go on to the roads; though, if we should come across a small one going our direction, it might be safe to go along the edge of it. The compass we had bought was a cheap German make, and the needle seemed to take an eternity before it stopped swinging. It was necessary to take a fresh bearing every few yards, for, often unable to see more than a few feet ahead, it proved almost impossible to maintain a straight line, and on many an occasion we found ourselves going due south instead of due west. It was often difficult to say whether a clump of bushes was a hill in the distance, or vice versâ. We would hold a whispered consultation and creep on. We still had one umbrella left, and the front man would feel his way with this, and the other would hold on to the tail of his coat.

In this manner we stumbled across Northern Germany.

CHAPTER XIX

BURGLARY

IN THE DAYS that followed I became extremely addicted to stealing. In the long hours that we spent lying hid under the branches of a tree that dripped on to us for the twenty hours that we sheltered beneath its branches, I would think of novel methods of burglary. I tried to think of articles of food that might be left about in some small cottage. Our first night had given us enough raw potatoes to last us for a day, allowing one a meal. They were still very young, but not so like a stone as they would be if older. I remember the peculiar sensation of that day. The day and night previous we had walked for very nearly twenty-three consecutive hours; hardly ever on the roads and over or through one obstacle and then another. We had eaten about five ounces of food. It had rained on and off during the whole time. Then at eight o'clock I was awakened from a sleep of utter exhaustion by the sun's rays penetrating the cold damp of my clothes. In the distance was the country spread out as a panorama before us. A pin point on the horizon, arising somewhat above its fellow hills, was the Dürenberg with its tower, which we had climbed the day before. On the other side of the horizons were the grey chimneys of the smelting furnaces of Osnabrück, which the night before we had seen belching forth great flames to the sky. We took our bearings with care, and reckoned that we must be on the top of the famous Peaceberg. We were much too far north. We might find ourselves on the plain, which would prove dangerous. That night we must go south-west, so as to make compensation for our northerly tendency. Our whole journey was a series of compromises between north and south. We were making for a point where the Teutoburger hills, beginning to peter out, touch the Ems-Dortmund Canal. Whenever we came up against an obstacle that necessitated our going one way or the other, the question would always arise: Are we too much north or too much south? It was impossible to gain any indication from the hills, as they ran in all directions without any method.

We just lay there, enjoying the warm sun as it mixed with the smell of bracken, heather, and pine. We wondered what our friends in Ruhleben were saying about us. We both agreed as the sun got warmer that, even if we were caught, the long months of solitary would never wipe out the memory of our four days' perfect holiday.

As we lay there in the afternoon, we suddenly heard a whole hurricane of voices. They came closer, and we could hear they were children. They would climb nearer to us, see us, and would then tell their mothers they had seen two strangers lying in the heather. The mothers, we prayed, would slap them soundly for telling lies, but the children would corroborate each other's statements, and the parents, now thoroughly alarmed, would all rush to the police, who, having that day received a description of two escaped prisoners from Ruhleben, would not hesitate to start a hunt with the assistance of the whole neighbourhood. For more than an hour they were all around us, shrieking to each other to come here and go there. They were picking bilberries, and we were right in the midst of a bush simply peppered with them. "It's all right," whispered Falk. "I'll talk to them, and they'll go away." They came within a few feet of us. "Got many bilberries, Elsa?" said Falk very quietly. The child looked round, startled, and on seeing us put its finger in its mouth and giggled. "Well, Gretel, and what about you? Have you got many?" and she also put a finger in her mouth and giggled like the first. Before he had exhausted his list of names we had in front of us a whole row of giggling children.

When they had gone, we decided that, though they seemed very satisfactorily disposed of, we had better move on, in case they should come back with a grown-up. When our trek was finished, and we were comfortably installed in a thicket a few hundred yards on, we found the only remaining umbrella had been left behind. We went back carefully, but could not find it. Our last protection against the rain was gone.

It was our habit to start walking at ten o'clock, by which time the last trace of daylight had disappeared from the sky, and all good peasant folk were abed. The three hours previous to starting, as light and noise gradually faded away, were times when the body and soul were absorbed in the one wish for warmth and food. Every day at seven o'clock the sky would grow darker, and for a couple of hours the cold rain would penetrate the light summer clothing, leaving us numbed and stiff for the start at ten.

That night, the fifth since our escape, we crossed over the crest of the Peaceberg, and stumbled down through the heather and pine on the other side. At the bottom we found a narrow grass path. The path went rather too much south for our liking, but we followed it, nevertheless, intending to compensate for it by following any track going too much to the north. We had eaten all the raw potatoes we had gathered the day before, and even with the one slice of cheese and the one prong's worth of sausage, it was still insufficient with which to undergo such a strain.

Henceforward we made it our duty to replenish our larder and our water-bottle at the first opportunity that presented itself. We found that the path led to a cottage. Burglary was my specialty, so, leaving Falk in the trees, with great caution I went forward to the hunt. The idea that I always followed on these occasions was the Red Indian dictum that anything that moves is twice as easily seen as anything still. Every pace or so, I would stop, and keep perfectly rigid for a few seconds, and then once more move on. I spent several minutes in opening the garden gate without noise. In the distance a dog was barking. I could just distinguish some tall rows of scarlet runners, and I got in between them to feel if there were any beans upon them. The fact that there was nothing forced me to go on and investigate the rest of the garden. Soon I found a row of plants, the nature of which I could not even guess at, but before long I found potatoes, and, after scratching up half a dozen and carefully replacing the stems in the holes made, I stole carefully back. I got into the lane, and before long I heard Falk's soft whisper, "Is that you?" Without realising it, I had been away forty minutes. Burglary is the most absorbing work imaginable. Every instant you are ready to see an irate owner in a night-cap issue forth, shouting and bellowing, and then comes the great moment when one has to decide whether to crouch down with not a finger moving, as rigid as a rock, every particle of white, even one's hands, covered up, trusting to luck that he will not see you, or whether to bolt as hard as possible into the darkness, trusting to luck that he will not catch you. Every nerve is strained and ready, and I believe that a feeling of the most perfect bliss will spread itself through the being of the merest tyro.

The greatest skill was needed a couple of nights after this, when, after having failed to get any water for some time, suddenly, out of the darkness, we could hear a slight dripping. We had imagined that there was not a house in the midst of such a dense forest as we were in. Falk sat down, and I crept forward á la Red Indian. Down beneath I could just perceive a small forester's cottage, and it was obvious that there was a tub somewhere to store the rainwater from the roof. I stood there, trying to make up my mind as to exactly where was the water-barrel before I attempted to descend the bank. In the dark I had underestimated the steepness, and had gone down it face first, to discover half-way down that the only practicable method was to go down backwards. If I should take another pace and slip, the door of the cottage, which was but a few yards away, right opposite where I was, would open, and, unable to hide or to run, I should be caught red-handed stealing up to this lonesome cottage. Being a wood-keeper's cottage, the owner would probably come out with a gun. I found it impossible to turn round, and that the bank was too steep to go up backwards. I began to feel rather like when I had been arrested, that something very terrible was going to happen within a few seconds: that within a moment or so I should be in another state of consciousness. For a quarter of an hour I stood there, making tentative movements in one direction after another, retracing each as the feeling that I was just about to fall became too great. Gradually, as it became necessary to do something, I let myself gently down on my heels, and suddenly taking my hands away from the ground beside me, I stretched them above my head, and, taking a firm grip of the grass above, lifted up my legs, and found resting-place for them lower down. Eventually I arrived noiselessly at the bottom, and found the water-butt. And as I filled the water-bottle, I could hear the connubial snores through the window-pane opposite me. Not even the gurgle of the water rushing into the water-bottle stopped them, and I climbed up the bank to rejoin Falk with a renewed sense of confidence.

As the black of the sky turned to an obscure grey, we came upon an opening in the woods. At first it seemed to be a larger forester's cottage, and then we saw it to be a chapel standing solitary in the centre of this wooded wilderness. There were no houses near, and any who came to attend its services must needs walk far. A long glade led away from it and down a hill. The door was open, even at three o'clock in the morning. We stayed and watched it from the shade of the trees, expecting somebody to come out, wishing we dared go in. Whether it was a ruin, or whether it was the object of a priest's care we never knew, for we left it, and going down the glade came out into cornfields. In the north-east the sky was beginning to get lighter. It was full time for us to hide.

Almost as soon as we had discovered a small copse in which to hide, and had broken down a small tree to act as a pillow, a storm broke, and lashed us with a fury we had not yet had to suffer. It immediately broke through the covering which the small fir trees provided, and though we covered our heads with our hats and capes, it beat us till we groaned with the cold. It was not yet light, and hours of agony followed. Too tired, too wretched and too weak to do anything to keep warm, it was yet too cold to sleep. Feet and hands were so numb that they felt nothing that touched them.

At midday the rain stopped, and we slept for an hour or two.

CHAPTER XX
A CORPSE

As WE PROCEEDED we found it difficult to distinguish the nights we had spent in the open. Often we would have long discussions as to which day of the week it was, spending hours trying to affix names to the sameness of the various copses we had spent daylight in. We always avoided any towns that lay in our route, and directly we saw their glare in the sky, we turned south or north. Our route, we knew, lay by Iburg and between Tecklenburg and Lengerich. For four nights we had been within sight of the great furnace fires that burnished the sky above Osnabrück, for our progress had not been more than four miles a night. The weak heart which I had developed from illness in Ruhleben, combined with the lack of food, was telling heavily upon me, and I was every day becoming weaker. We were still about forty-five miles from the frontier, even as the crow flies. Our experience had taught the bitter lesson that going across country by night necessitates covering two or three times as much distance as the crow flies. As the food was running shorter we had taken to raw mangel-wurzels, turnips and sugar beets. When cut up into thin slices they were quite palatable, but after eating a certain amount, the throat becomes very dry, and it is impossible to eat more. The saving fact about them was that they contained sugar. We had brought with us tins of meat extract and some Horlick's milk tablets. The meat seemed to have no effect, but the milk tablets, if we had only had enough, would have carried us through the whole fortnight that we spent in this fashion. As it was, we ate but few of them, meaning to keep them for the last iron reserve. Curiously enough, I felt neither intense hunger nor intense thirst, but simply an overpowering weakness. We had two drinks of water a day, and this seemed sufficient.

One night, when we had both forgotten to wind our watches, we started earlier than we intended. Falk had climbed down a bank to a stream which we had detected by the sound of some cows drinking at it, when I suddenly perceived a female figure coming towards me. I moved as quickly and as quietly as I could behind a tree, but as I did so, I feared she had seen me. At that moment Falk came staggering up the bank, with the water-bottle, and ran straight into her arms. They were both within a yard or two of me. The woman was just hidden by a few branches that came between us. For a moment there was a silence, and then Falk, with his usual presence of mind, took the offensive. "Confound the thing," he said, "the cork won't go in. Ah, that's it," and he fumbled with the water-bottle. "It's a fine night, isn't it?" It had been pouring with rain two hours before. "Hullo, you needn't be frightened of me. What do you think I am? Oh, so you thought I was going to steal your cows. Well, there they are, quite safe. Good night to you." And he walked on.

The woman stood there, doing nothing, and I could see

her head against the sky, and could notice the way her hair was piled up. She was still a couple of feet away, and I could hear her breathing nervously. She seemed to have no intention of moving, obviously staying there to protect her cows from me. Her breathing grew louder. I could see that in a moment her nerve would go, and she would emit a piercing scream and fall fainting through the branches into my arms. She would revive, and thinking I was going to murder her, would die of fright at my feet. And I should stand where I was then, immovable from mere habit, with a female corpse at my feet. It was necessary that something should be done. Very gently I began the futile proceeding of making a soft hissing noise through my teeth, as if I was ascending the steep bank from the stream, and found it an effort. We both of us knew we were within touching distance of one another, and that the other knew it also, but this seemed a way of getting out of the impasse, and at the same time saving each other's faces. It was simply out of the question to come out from behind that bush as if I was a naughty little schoolboy found in a situation necessitating explanations. When my panting finally reached a climax, and I stepped forth with a hasty good night, she said not a word, but wrapping her cloak around her went off in the opposite direction to which I did.

I found Falk waiting for me a little further on, and we both agreed that it was still too early. Nevertheless there was at that point no good cover, so we were forced to go forward in a state of expectation. Our chief fear from the very beginning was that, forced by the nature of the terrain into taking to the road, we should meet a bicycling gendarme who would ask us for papers. Another couple who had escaped from the hospital at Ruhleben in April had separated, and one man had been caught at Cloppenburg, north of Osnabrück, in this manner, and the other had been shot while attempting to cross the frontier. That night, after the episode of the woman and her cows, the lack of cover, and the nature of the ground keeping us for a considerable time upon the road, which did not run exactly in the direction we wanted, was a great strain, though it had a compensation in store for us.

We had both expected that the bridges over the Ems-Dortmun Canal, the Ems itself, and the River Vechte would all be strongly guarded, and that we should be forced to swim them. We had put down on the list of things to buy in Berlin, but had forgotten to do so, a pair of "sea-wings," on which to float the kit, or rather more especially the collapsible cooker and its few lumps of solid spirit. Suddenly, there was a sharp turn of the road, and we found ourselves practically on a bridge. It was far too suspicious a thing to do to go back, even if there were sentries, and if there weren't, it mattered not going forward. On the right and left through the great steel girders was the canal, with its great stone sides stretching away into the darkness. As we lay beneath the dripping trees of a small copse a few hours later, we agreed that Prussian organisation was much overrated.

On the next night my friend nearly left me. We were trudging across a moor of deep spring heather, occasionally enlivened by great spaces of soft sand, and I was endeavouring to keep Falk in view, despite the fact that he seemed to be dancing on his head, and doing all sorts of odd things with his legs, when I gave a little squeal and dropped dead. Falk heard me and turned around. He shouted at me; he felt for my pulse, but could find nothing. He tore open my shirt, and tried to listen to my heart; he could hear nothing.

He kicked me hard time after time, till he became convinced that it was all over, and that for me this was the end of the great trek. He looked up and saw the day was just beginning to break. It was essential to hide, for we were now only twenty-five to thirty miles away from the frontier. It was silly to stay there beside a useless corpse, and it would no longer do me any good. He glanced down at me once more, and then went plodding on over the heather...

Now this versatile friend of mine included in his Nigerian duties of district commissioner that of sheriff, and one of his many duties as sheriff was to certify the death of murderers condemned to death. Not being a medical man, he had made his one criterion the fact of the jaw dropping— or not—as the case might be; and as he trudged over the spongy heather towards Holland, the doubt suddenly tumbled into his mind as to whether the jaw of that corpse he had left behind had dropped or not. For the life of him he could not remember. He tore back, jumping over great bushes of heather, his Loden cloak flying off his shoulders behind him, first thinking that it had been one way and then the other, to find the jaw shut and just a flicker making its appearance in my eyelids.

One impression followed another so rapidly that though it seemed impossible that the memory of it should ever go, yet the succeeding one invariably obliterated it, and so I have left nothing but the last. The day after we crossed the first bridge has completely faded from my memory. All I know is that I lay in some undergrowth, wet and cold, but too weak even to shiver. I remember thinking that my chances of getting through to the frontier were almost nil, and that I was not in the least disturbed by the idea, but thankful that the nights, and days too, of effort would now soon end. It was not in me to wish I had not tried to come, just as I could not wish that I had not breathed the last breath. I remember Falk woke me up at four, soon after the sky was light, and gave me our one daily drink of hot cocoa. I remember he woke me up at lunch to give me the sausage and the slip of cheese: that I was too indifferent to things to protest against his giving me more than my share. I remember the usual cold douche of rain when the sun set, and that after that I could not feel my body. I remember his saying it was nine o'clock, and that in an hour we must start, and I remember the question in his voice. Otherwise, the twenty hours we passed there did not exist for me.

As ten o'clock approached, I knew that I must pull myself to my feet, and I made up my mind to make one more effort at any rate. Before we started we divided up the food, in case I dropped again, and Falk should not bring me to life again before daylight. Neither of us felt in the least tragic about this possibility. It was an ever-present fact, a companion to our thoughts, whom we discussed dispassionately and with the contempt of familiarity.

That night I had to rest at the end of every twenty minutes, but despite this, we covered nearly nine miles. The country was now much easier. Instead of high hills across our path at every mile, the land was as flat as the Dutch fens we were daily approaching. Pine trees and long ditches were of what, by experience, we decided the landscape consisted. We found a small grass path running parallel to the road, which had a north-west direction. This suited us well, for we had wandered too far south. We expected the road to lead to Emsdetten, just before which there was a bridge over the Ems. As the canal bridge, which is vastly more important, was not guarded, we did not expect the Ems bridge to be. In this we were right, but as we crossed it we thanked our stars that we had not had to swim it, for at this point the river is immensely broad, very slow and sluggish, and is shallow with a mud bottom. It was plain that I, at any rate, would never have got across it alive.

That night, almost for the first time, we went through a town. We dreaded lest there should be "night watchmen," but Emsdetten was short of men. I noticed a shop window filled with the most extraordinary objects, which I surmised were ladies' hats. I looked desperately for an automatic chocolate-machine, and in preparation I searched in my trousers pocket for ten-pfennige pieces. They were not needed, for the place seemed denuded of anything approaching even an automatic machine of any sort if it ever had any. We met no night-watchmen; only a solitary dog and another pair of osculatory lovers, who fled at our approach, crossed our path as we padded on towards Holland. We were unable to get much further that night, for the heavy rains had made the sandy country into a quagmire of heavy mud. We finished the night's walk about four miles out of Emsdetten.

It was the eighteenth of July. It was eleven days ago that we started. It was strange that it should seem weeks, if not months ago since that night we had stood on each side of a wire-netting fence, every moment expecting the shout of a sentry, every heartbeat throbbing in our ears, and almost as yesterday the day we had first decided that we must escape, that Ruhleben was unbearable. Time and space assumed gigantic and microscopic proportions. We had covered fifty miles, and the next ten seemed impossible of accomplishment. We had been nine days on the road, and it seemed as if the sun would never rise.

The strain was beginning to tell even on Falk, whose

long treks in Nigeria had partially accustomed him to such trials. We were forced to the admission that the escape was becoming reduced to an impasse for want of food, and that a coup was necessary for its solution. Hitherto, we had had under four ounces of food—as apart from raw turnips and mangel-wurzels—per diem, and though we were only about twenty miles away from the frontier, we should be forced to do the last portion so slowly, so carefully that we might have to reckon on doing no more than six to seven miles in the last three days. We had learnt our lesson, and we knew that three nights was not an excessive time when you stop every ten yards, when you may have to lie opposite a fence for a whole day and night, watching the sentries guarding it, before you make a stealthy dash. The situation was rendered more serious also by the fact that the soil this side of the Ems was so much richer that the potatoes grew at a depth to which it was impossible for torn fingernails and weak fingers to scratch. Falk decided to go back into Emsdetten that afternoon, and buy food. We licked and scraped him several times all over until he was clean. We had brought a small safety razor and lump of soap with us, and he shaved himself until he reached respectability. Then he made his way out of the copse after remarking, "If I'm not back in three or four hours, you must crawl on as best you can." "All right," I replied, "you'll get caught right enough. See you in prison later. All the same, best luck to you." He disappeared into the road, and I wondered whether I should see him again.

He marched down the road, meeting no one during the hour and a half it took him to reach Emsdetten. When he got into the town, he noticed what seemed to him an unusual number of women going about, and as he wondered at this he espied the dreaded gendarme standing at the cross-roads.

The latter turned round and looked at him, but he strode off down a side street towards the centre of the town, looking for a grocer.

All the shops were shut. It was a Catholic neighbourhood, and this was a saint's day. The crowd of well-dressed women had been women flocking to the church. All the risk of getting there, all the risk of getting back, would have been taken for nothing. It was essential to have food. He walked on, looking lugubriously at his reflection in the drawn blinds of shop windows. He went on for the sake of something to do; he looked about him for the sake of the one drop of hope that the town might contain a single citizen who at the same time protested and grocered. Whenever he saw a side street he went down it, and his persistence was finally rewarded when he found a small shop kept by a buxom lady of about forty and much curiosity. His main purchase consisted of cheese, margarine, and beet sugar. He asked for sausage and meat of any sort, but the old lady said she was too poor to sell such expensive things nowadays. "Now what else can I buy?" he said, and waited for her suggestion. She replied—as he hoped, but thinking they might need a bread ticket had not dared to ask for—biscuits, so he purchased a few biscuits for his brother's children. "Now I want three pounds of solid chocolate," he said.

"Dear me," she remarked, enormously pleased, "what an extravagant man you are."

"Yes," he replied promptly, "aren't I, but this, you see, is for my fiancée."

It is the custom in Prussian to give continual presents to the beloved one, and chocolate is a substance quite commonly employed for such purposes. "How is it you have not been taken for the army? My man has," she asked, as she began doing up the purchases.

"Oh," he replied, "worse luck, I am unfit."

"Where are you working?" she continued.

"On the Burgsteinfurt-Rheine Canal," he remarked, "and I thought, since I was passing through Emsdetten, I would make the weekly purchases here."

Without a second's hesitation she returned to the attack. "Burgsteinfurt-Rheine Canal," she remarked, "where is that? I've never heard of it."

"*Never heard* of the Burgsteinfurt-Rheine Canal," he said, "and you lived here all these years?"

"No. Well now, how should I? I am a poor woman and I've got six children. I don't have time to go out." And then she purred into Falk's sympathetic ear expostulations and complaints till the last knot on the parcel had been tied and the change counted twice over.

Just as I was beginning to think he had been caught, Falk broke through the branches into the copse, staggering triumphantly with the weight of a huge parcel. He had altogether got nine pounds, which meant that if we allowed another week or six days, we should each have about twelve ounces of food per day.

That night, as we stumbled out of a wood, we came across the Burgsteinfurt-Rheine Canal. It had been filled up, we could see, years ago.

CHAPTER XXI
GUNPOWDER AND CAVALRY

WITH A GOOD ROAD, an early start, and a good breakfast, in ordinary times we could have been in Holland from where we lay within one day. With a bicycle we could have done it in a couple of hours. The train covers the distance day after day in less than half an hour, and an aeroplane could do it in fifteen minutes. According to our reckoning, based on retrospection, four days would be the minimum time in which we could hope to get over the twenty miles that lay between us and the first few yards of Dutch soil. As a matter of fact, it was five days before we covered the last mile.

We were both happy that now at last we were coming to a decision. The extra food had made me stronger, and in addition Falk had sacrificed some of his share, in order that I might not find the strain too great. He also carried nearly all the weight of the kit. He chose the route, and made out our position from the scrap of map we had left. As we passed through the land we tore off that part of the map, in case there should be fortresses on it that we might be accused of spying on, should we be caught. There was nothing he did not do, from standing above me with a stop-watch at the regular twenty-minute rest, to helping me along over tough parts of the route. Though the weather got still worse, I got better as every day went past. Nevertheless, it was still a terrible effort to keep up. For four days more after Falk's daring return into Emsdetten, we lay in one copse after another, with but little difference between any of them. For four nights we struggled over flat water-logged country till our legs felt like pendulums swung backwards and forwards by heavy weights attached to their ends. Sometimes exasperation would attack us simultaneously, and we would both become careless of the noise we made, or even go so far as to walk upon a road and risk a bicycling gendarme. Sometimes we would meet figures like ourselves, cloaked, with head bent down to avoid the lashing of the rain, pushing forward through the mud, splashing recklessly through the puddles, absorbed in their own aches and pains, but with hopes of warmth and home at their journey's end. It was when desire to get along quicker had overcome our principle of taking every precaution we could think of and had produced a "damn-the-consequences" frame of mind, that we were led into a fix that made us forswear all temptation of that sort for the future. We were walking along a road that, even in the dark, seemed of fair importance, when suddenly through the trees on each side we saw the twinkling of lamps. There was noise that the rain prevented us from defining. It was impossible to say how far away the lights were. Keeping well to the side of the road, and treading as quietly as possible, we continued. The noise grew louder. It seemed to be an engine in some factory. Suddenly the road turned and broadened out, and great arc lamps on each side blinded us. The throbbing of the engine was now a roar. We caught sight of the well-known landsturm uniform quite close.

Without a word to each other, we strode forward, knowing instinctively it to be our only hope. Great fences of barbed wire, the tallest I had ever seen, lined the road, and behind them were little huts with bright lights that spread in rows into the distance. On each side was a huge iron gate, and as we passed the two sentries, with their bayonets gleaming on the tops of their rifles, rolled lazily towards us. "Good evening," we mumbled, as restraining ourselves, we walked on.

But we had hardly passed them and had left them rolling back into the shelter of their boxes, when a railway crossing, with gates shut, barred the road. A porter was taking down the lights from a signal. We were brought to a standstill. Something went wrong with the mechanism for lowering the lamps. I began to think now nice it would be to have one of them to take with us. It seemed funny to be waiting there, not far from Holland, and the German sentries a little way down the road, waiting for a porter to unlock a barrier for us. I began wondering what would happen if the sentries and the signal lamps were to change places, if a red lamp was placed on the muddy ground at the factory gate, and if the sentries were to loll nonchalantly on the spike at the head of the signal post, shouting to trains they were to stop and go on. It wasn't in the least exciting, waiting there in the glare of those lights in the sight of the sentry with the gas engine pounding and the signal creaking and clattering. The porter said nothing, but went on manipulating the wheel at the foot of the signal. We waited, not quite knowing what to do. Finally he got his lamp down, and unhooked, and then, gruffly apologising, lifted the barrier and bade us good night. We strolled on. In twenty minutes' time, when we took our usual rest, we looked at the map and determined that by the favour of Fortune we had come straight through the well-known powder factory of Wettringen.[1]

I was wakened up at six o'clock, after three hours' sleep, by my friend prodding me sharply and whispering, "Get your legs in, you fool, get your legs in; there is a squadron of cavalry all around us"; and I drew my legs in under the fir tree and pressed myself still deeper into the gnarled roots of the heather. The sun was just beginning to make itself felt, and I was annoyed at having to draw my legs in from its warmth. All around me I could hear the swishing of horses' hoofs as they trotted and galloped through the heather, and a raucous and furious voice was shouting commands just a few yards away outside the copse. Again, the reader must believe me or not as he likes, there was nothing exciting about this. There was no dramatic suspense. If you were caught, you were caught, a truism that seemed to cover everything. The ground was still just as wet, the air just as cold, and the heather roots just as rough as before these gentlemen on horses made their presence heard. If somebody were to come through the sparsely treed copse and tread on us, the probability was that we should be noticed, and if he did, that would be the end of the matter; meanwhile, my eyelids were so heavy that I could not keep them open, and a coarse military voice mixed itself with a heather root that was sticking itself into my leg, in my dreamy ideas of what was going on in Europe during the next hour.

Later on I woke up slightly, and hovered between reality and dreams. The colonel, who was obviously a man of about

---

[1] I believe that this gunpowder factory has since been blown up as the result of a fire.

forty with an unlimited vocabulary, was instructing his flock as to how to carry out certain manœuvres. Towards the end of two hours, he grew slightly hoarse. Sometimes his voice would grow nearer and nearer, and then die away into the distance, and a minute later the whole squadron would gallop as hard as their horses could take them up to the edge of the copse and then stop dead. Numbers of times we though they were going to ride in, and my tired brain tried to think of answers to the questioning we should be subjected to when taken before the colonel, whom I was sure from the tone of his voice was a very stiff frightful Prussian, and had no back to his head. At the conclusion of one charge, when he had delivered his usual lecture, he began to explain the forth-coming manœuvre. Most of it was uninteresting until he said, "Section A will now send a man to see if this copse is clear of the enemy." "Dear, dear," I thought, "this means I've got to bury my face in that particularly stubbly chunk of heather just there; how distinctly uncomfortable. Here comes section A." And a bored young farmer, his belly encircled with a belt with "Gott mit uns" inscribed on it, sat on his horse while the latter carried him through the copse. He was carried in this manner about eight yards away from us, nonchalant and dreamy he passed away. I noticed the white mark on the leg of his horse, which was a beautiful jet-black beast. Had he been slightly more awake he would have seen us without fail; but directly he entered the copse his eyes sought only for a place where he might quit it.

At ten o'clock we saw them through the trees trotting away, and they never came back.

That night we went on again. The weather was rapidly becoming worse. Two nights later the wind rose to a perfect hurricane, with great sweeping waves of rain every half-hour or so. We were uncertain as to where we were. In Ruhleben we had determined to aim for a small nose of Dutch territory that juts into Germany at the point where the Westphalian and Hanoverian boundaries touch. On the north should be Bentheim and Schuttorf and on the south Ochtrup and Gronau. Roads would obviously join these towns and a small railway was also marked on the map between Gronau and Bentheim, and when we had crossed this we knew that the frontier would not be far off. We were attempting to go parallel and between two railway lines, one of which goes through Gronau, Ochtrup and on to the Dutch town of Enschede, and the other of which runs through Bentheim and on to Oldenzaal.

As we stumbled along, we saw to the north a slight reflection on the low-lying clouds which we hoped were the lights of Bentheim. Every night, but that night of all nights, when the march was gradually approaching its climax, we would stop every few paces and Falk would lean over the compass waiting for that eternal swinging to stop, give a short nod or point into the darkness, and we would go on keeping as straight as we could, due west. As we wandered on through small pine woods, obviously by their appalling regularity planted by a benevolent Government, we became more and more at a loss as to our position. We had expected to meet a main road going north and south, which would tell us that we had reached the longitude of Bentheim and Ochtrup, but to our horror we found road after road going north and south every kilometre, and a little later we found that a road also went west and east every kilometre. The whole country was divided up into square kilometres. These, we knew, though it helped us not a whit, were the great tracts of waste moor which the Government were reclaiming by means of prison labour. Huge ditches, almost small canals, cut up the land into interstices. Regular squares of regularly planted pine trees were alternated by heather land that was in the process of being converted into pasture. Our impression that night of all others was that the whole of Germany was a mass of barbed wire. There were, of course, no hedges in country such as this, but every hundred yards brought us up against a complicated barbed-wire fence, difficult to climb or to get underneath. It was common enough that we would both try getting through the strands at points a few yards apart, and simultaneously, with a leg each side of the bottom strand, and our heads almost touching it, our rücksacks would fix us rigidly to the upper one. Later, we became more expert at it, and would go through one by one, wasting much time, and in full view of any unseen watcher, but quicker than we had gone before. At times we would find ourselves looking down into a water-filled ditch, several yards wide, with a high bank of sand the other side, and as we scrambled up opposite the wind would take the splashing of the falling earth and carry it away for all to hear.

The overpowering weakness that had beset me almost a week ago, nearly leaving me alone, taken for dead, on a former heath twenty miles behind us, again began to steal over me, slowly paralysing every movement, numbing every sense, leaving untouched but one great mastering desire to leave off from further effort, to lie down and seek for rest and nothing else. It was not any dream of the tears of my sorrowing family, when the news trickled through that I had been shot or gone mad in a prison, that spurred me on to take yet another step, but the dancing image of a well-spread table, the first great meal that Amsterdam should give me, or even the coarse solidity of prison fare. It never occurred to me that when I should eventually reach one or the other, I should stare moodily at what was spread before me unable to eat more than our usual four ounces.

Gradually the barbed-wire fences grew fewer, and finally ceased altogether. The ditches, though less frequent, became larger and deeper. Soon there was a slight rise in the ground, which, though covered with rushes, grew dryer for a time. In the distance was a faint lightness in the sky. It was nearly one o'clock. The sun would rise in an hour and a half, and we must find a hiding-place other than this heather before that time. We were forced to resort to continual rests, which we had been able to abandon for a couple of nights, and every twenty minutes found me lying a huddled heap in the heather, with the one wish that the last of the ten minutes might never come. In a few minutes the earth again began to grow spongy in parts, and it became even harder to go on. I remember keeping my eyes on Falk, and wondering why one should walk on one's feet instead of one's hands. I remember an odd passage coming back to me from a book that had excited me greatly when at school. I remember feeling that my collar was tight. Every now and then a pile of earth would rise up a few feet from the ground, and a few square yards would lie barren, stripped of its heather and its soil. The air was fresh, and the rain had been blown away for the time by the wind. A white path would sometimes cross our way, and a silvery splash would seem to be water till it was tried and proved to be sand. Ever in the distance was this faint light, and we were uncertain whether it was the lights of Ochtrup or the moon shining dimly through the clouds.

Suddenly everything changed for me. I felt my heart give a sickening leap, as if it would break itself against my ribs, and the sky and heath had disappeared. Great masses of earth were being hurled about, and one hit my head so that it almost fell off my neck. I found myself lying crumpled up in a pool of mud, looking up at the frayed edges of a pit. I got myself on my feet, and reached up. I could just get my head over the edge. I called to Falk to come and help me out, but the wind was blowing hard in the wrong direction. I got into the corner, for it was cut square and like a large room, and in five minutes had scrambled out. Falk, of course, was nowhere to be seen. I thought I heard the echo of my own voice calling him. He had the compass tied round his neck, and though I had one also, it was not luminous, and it was impossible to light a match. I remembered that the light in the sky lay roughly in our route, and I prayed that it had not altered its position as I went on. Then I heard Falk calling, and I called back, trying to locate him. I pounded over the heather in all directions and when I asked him where he was, he answered "Here," and told me to come quickly. I rushed towards where the voice seemed to come, and found Falk unable to move, gradually sinking ever deeper into a morass. Fortunately I found a piece of hard ground near enough to throw him the rope that we always carried round our waists, which we had made from our ball of string.

We were both somewhat exhausted by this, and when we were sitting on some lumps of peat Falk remarked: "I know whereabouts we are now. We have come over the Brechte, and now we are on the Gildenhauser Venner."

Some time in the eighteenth century an English ambassador was returning from Vienna to Rotterdam, where he intended to take a boat for England. His route lay across the Gildenhauser Venner. He stopped at a village to change horses, and while this was being done, stepped a few paces forward into the darkness. He has never been heard of since. For a long time foul play was suspected, but afterwards it was acknowledged he had been swallowed by one of the quagmires.

As there was not the faintest possibility of telling what was safe and what was not, we went straight ahead. Often soft white would prove to be softer still beneath, and the hard sand would billow and heave as we walked across it expecting a sudden rend to drop through the bottomless and almost liquid slime. Sometimes it would look safer to go forward to a black patch that must be hard in the midst of all this white, but which our feet would tread into and find still less resistant, and we would quickly throw ourselves back, wondering if all the world be like this. Sometimes a long stretch of hard ground would tempt us to believing there was no more soft quagmire yet to come. But we knew better by the time a road rose up out of the darkness and a small pine wood offered shelter to us on the other side.

It was two o'clock, but the thick clouds kept it dark as midnight and gave us time to creep on yet nearer to the frontier. We found a small road and followed it till it turned too much north, when we broke off across the fields. Presently we came across a small stream. This puzzled us, for it seemed to be flowing in the wrong direction if our map was right. True we had found it to be out of date before; but then it had some excuse. Perhaps there had been an earthquake since. We stood in the shadow of the trees talking.

We had crossed the stream and were in a pine wood of tall trees. There was undergrowth and they were thinly planted. We had crossed over a bridge of fantastic white woodwork and had found ourselves in this wood, which we decided to be a gentleman's park. There was probably a house near. We went with a care that we had never exercised before, for we knew that we were within three miles of the frontier, and it was quite likely, after our experience of the cavalry squadron, that there were several cordons before the frontier was reached. The wind had dropped, and there was a great quiet in the wood. Soon there would be light, and even as we looked upwards the tree tops stood out clear against the sky. It was impossible to hide here. I led the way, for my sight and ears were keener.

Every ten paces we would stop and listen. We could never hear anything, but we always did stop nevertheless. At every step we tried to think how we might put our feet down quieter at the next. I could feel my friend take hold of the tail of my cloak. It was very intense, for as I felt my way from one tree to another, with first one hand stretched out in front and then the other, I never knew whether my fingers would touch a sentry or if I might have the luck possibly to touch his rifle first. The idea came to me that I might touch it so gently that he would not notice it, and then I should stand still, trying not to complete the step I should be in process of taking, trying not to breathe, willing that he should not see me, my other hand communicating to Falk not to ask me what was wrong, but just to stand like a rock, patiently and in ignorance, until inch by inch we three should be feet apart——

I remember I thought of a Birmingham metal factory. I forgot how my thoughts travelled there, and then pell-mell after one another, thoughts of a motor-'bus, Devonshire cream, the Chamonix valley, a line from a verse of Browning ending "where Alp meets Heaven in snow," Raffles, my rooms at Cambridge, the future of Eugenics and a banana tumbled into my brain as I racked and strained myself to listen and to see, and with the tips of my outstretched fingers to feel more keenly and more sensitively...

The wood came to an end. There was a road. On the other side the wood recommenced. The stream by our side went under the road and on through the next wood. It was nearly daylight. We waited.

As we crawled over on hands and knees, I noticed that to a point further down the road I must be showing up against the white woodwork bridge. One notices things like this on occasions like those. I said to myself that when it came to the real thing to-morrow night, there must be no carelessness of this sort. Little did I know what was in store for me for the next night.

We could see through the wood now and hurried on as quick as silence permitted. There seemed to be nowhere to hide. We were feverish as we looked form one place to another. We saw a few trees, hardly enough to call a clump, but that had low-spreading branches, and by them a small pond, almost a puddle. We were hoping for better. We found nothing, and there was a red-roofed cottage the other side. The light was becoming stronger every minute. A dog was barking in the distance ahead of us. We went back and crawled underneath the branches of the fir tree, which dripped wet on us. It was half-past three. I fell asleep.

I had been rather garrulous all day. It was rather a luxurious day. We had decided that henceforward all the kit, with the exception of the ropes, must be left behind. The ropes we had made into loops, so that if there were fences we should run at them, slip these loops over the top of the poles and pray that we might get over before the sentry appeared and had time to shoot. The cooker we mournfully decided must go also. Therefore, with unprecedented extravagance we decided that we would have three hot meals that day to use up what was left of the spirit, for to-morrow we might be dead. The day was spent in measuring the time since the last drink of cocoa to when the next was due. We ran short of water, and during a hailstorm I crawled down on my belly, taking particular care to keep out of the view of the little red cottage, to the puddle which had by now sunk into the marshy surrounding. It had obviously been a pond quite lately, for it was a large basin, and there was viscid slime all the way from the edge. I found when I had crawled through this that there was not enough water to fill the water-bottle, and also that the basin was deep enough for me to stand up. The hail beat me furiously. I jumped on the water-bottle and stamped it into the mud. Water trickled into it but slowly.

Near by we could hear church bells ringing. "They must be the bells of Gronau," we decided. "We can't be more than a couple of kilometres from the frontier now."

At sundown we heard a thundering soldier's marching chorus break through the air. "The new guard coming on duty," we remarked grimly. "There sounds enough of them. Looks cheerful for to-night."

I was talking about what I was going to do in London three days hence, and how I thought I might as well write a book if I could but remember all that had happened, and we interrupted this chatter to cover up the saucepan under the leaves and to throw away our small coin in case it should chink, in preparation for the last dash through the German lines, on which we would start in an hour's time. I was continuing where I left off, as to what I would do in England with my new-found life, and Falk was getting more and more frightened at my tempting of Providence, imploring me to stop and remember that there was yet the hardest to do, and I had laughed softly to myself with the pleasure of my dream, and was dreaming it out loud once again, when I heard a crackle. Falk remarked that one of his teeth had broken, and said he had forgotten the feel of a tooth brush. I recommended him a dentist in London. I finished a few sentences of the dream, and lay still thinking of London. A twig cracked immediately behind my ear, and instead of turning round, I put my hand up to my hat, which was fixed in the twigs, and holding it steady, turned my head round inside its brim... Behind me, so close that I noticed the texture of his trousers, was a soldier, who was holding aside the branches and stooping down over us. He was smiling slightly...

"It's all up," I whispered softly to Falk, "here's the guard." Falk turned lazily over on his elbow, half thinking I was joking. The soldier neither moved nor spoke. None of us said a word. There was a long silence.

My eyes lost the power of focussing, and I looked through the grey uniform, and beyond I could see a prison cell and a man sitting in it, his hands between his knees: an expressionless face. The walls were green and shiny, and high up on them was a dark green band. The window had five bars. The man never moved. I saw my future before me; there seemed no ending to it.

"Well, Herr Doktor," Falk was saying to me in a loud voice, "it's about time we were going on." He turned to the soldier. "It's a bit late, isn't it?" he remarked. For a few moments the soldier said nothing...

Then he said, "What are you doing here?"

Falk began the usual story of our being Wandervögel, which did all very well for the Harz mountains, but was a remarkably thin story with which to be on the Dutch frontier. The way it was received seemed to me exactly like telling a lie at school, and not being very successful, until a full stop is reached in the middle of a sentence, and you wait for the verdict. I remember thinking that Falk would have to be extremely ingenious to account for our lying on ground that squelched as we turned on it. I made no effort to assist him, for I nearly cried aloud with the desire that we might get through the arrest as quickly as possible. I had been through it once already. As I numbly gazed at the man, I ached with the thought that I was nothing but a fatuous dreamer after all; that it was impossible for anybody ever to escape the great arm of Prussian organisation; that I might have known they'd catch us here. I noticed that he was very slow for a German soldier, until I saw that his rifle was slung across his back. Then it struck me that he thought we were very desperate, and would get up and fall upon him if he made any attempt to arrest us. He and Falk were still talking. He spoke the vile dialect of the neighbourhood, and I found it hard to understand what he said.

Suddenly he changed the subject, and said, "Do you know that you are on Dutch soil?"

"No! no!" I said loudly, galvanised by what I thought was an obvious trick to make us avow ourselves. "Nothing of the sort."

He addressed something more in his wretched speech to Falk, and my friend in his excitement, jumping up, took him by the lapels of his coat and shook him, saying, "No, we are not really in Holland, not really?" And then we knew we really must be in Holland, that he really must be a Dutchman, for no German soldier would let you shake him violently by the lapels of his coat.

Without knowing it, we had come through the German sentries and their cavalry patrol the night before. The road we had crawled over as general precaution was their line, was the Real Thing after all. We were fifty feet over the frontier and behind us through the thin belt of trees were the German sentries. The bells we had heard ringing had been the bells of Enschede.

And as we walked down a rough country land at the end of which, not far away, was England, our jolly Dutch frontier guard, who had taken us for smugglers, said, "You see that red-roofed cottage over there?"

"I should think I do," I replied, "I've been crawling about on my belly in mud all day, in order to keep out of its sight."

"Well," he remarked, "it's been a close thing for you. That cottage is in Holland. The rain from its roof drips off into Germany."

EDITOR'S EPILOGUE

Unknown to Pyke when he wrote this book, fellow conspirator Wallace Ellison followed him out of Ruhleben thirteen days later, bolting from a work detail on July 23, 1915. Pyke and Falk had considered it too dangerous to ride trains near the Dutch border, but that is precisely what Ellison did, covering the entire distance in one day—arriving there, in fact, the same day as Pyke and Falk did. As predicted, he was immediately arrested by German border guards and sent back to Ruhleben. He escaped again—successfully, this time—in November 1917.

The Ruhleben racecourse, the site of the internment camp, no longer exists. It was torn down in 1958 and is now a sewage treatment plant.

— P.C.

Map of Route from Ruhleben to the Duch Frontier

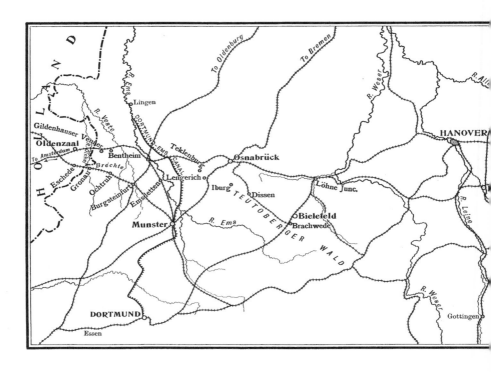

SCALE OF BRITISH MILES

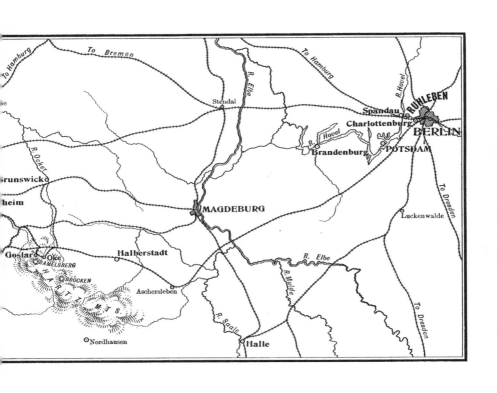